IN THE
ENVELOPE
OF
MEMORY

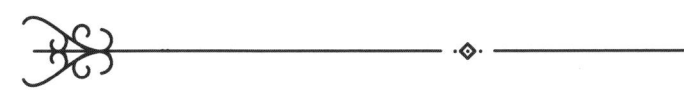

ILANA HALEY

CONTENTS

FORWARD BY JOHN BRUSSEAU

WHAT IS IT THAT TAKES A WOMAN EIGHTY plus years to understand, to unravel, to sort out? How is it that she can live an entire life and still need to review the patterns that replayed over and over, patterns begun in childhood and morphed into the long series of relationships that followed her all through adulthood?

These clippings now, at the closing years of life, pulled from the envelope of Ilana Haley's memory, are played like cards from a most winsome deck. They tell both Ilana and us the answer to these questions dipped in sorrow and wonder. They speak to us the riddle of un-faced early childhood conflicts and early childhood dependency, by a father, on a daughter, for emotional support, early templates for every relationship that would come to Ilana's willing and adventurous soul. These clippings from Ilana's mental envelope reveal these mirrored templates in the stories of other members of Ilana's early life. This is a book caught on the edge of a life's great challenge. It has the importance, the meaningfulness, of a story spun from the autonomous unconscious mind of a person for the spiritual (there really is no better word for it) purpose of aiding Ilana in making sense of the precious, the anguished, the sweet, the fulfilled, the unrequited, even the trauma-filled moments of her life. And as we read this correspondence from Ilana's inner mentor we are given an invitation to discover the meaning of our own life.

You cannot possibly read this book without simultaneously reviewing your life's meaning and purpose, and that is what a book such as this one is for. It is a spiritual trigger, provoking you to seek out the meaning of life, of your life and its moments stored in the envelope of your own memory. Don't be surprised when this happens, and remind yourself along the way to pour yourself into this self-reflective adventure. Engage this process with gusto. After all, you have your own inner Ilana Haley to satisfy.

CHAPTER 1

Flight

PANIC TOOK HOLD OF ME ON THE AIRPLANE. On my right, Helen held my hand, as she kept moving her gentle, white fingers over my forehead, insisting: Calm down, girl. Take it easy! For a moment it was not so bad, passing like a dream through a mist of dull pain: her fingertips with their fluttering pulse. After a while, I lay down between the seats on the floor of the plane. It was hard, cold and harrowing ... I returned to my seat, my heart was still booming like the jet engines; and again Pearl urged, as she gently massaged my temples with her cool fingers, which dripped with gold and diamonds: Calm down, take it easy girl;. for a moment I sank deeply within myself...

Teddy was not at home when I arrived. I was so exhausted from the flight, returning to Boston, that all I could do was to drop everything and collapse on the bed fully clothed. I didn't even hear

Teddy when he came home, although I did imagine that I felt as if a butterfly's wings are touching my cheek.

I was dreaming of you, Ora, my beloved friend. I dreamt I woke up in my small room in Boston to find you, winking down at me from your paintings on the walls, enveloping me in your aura. The clown painting on the wall looks at me with curious eyes. What's wrong, he asks. I do not know what to say. With tortured eyes, suddenly he seems old, tired. A girl is gazing into the distance – her eyes full of blue longing; a dove hovers above her airy fingers. Three women, one faceless, are looking at me in surprise – Well? I don't know, I answer, turning away in shame. Faceless laughs placidly: You know, she whispers. The two lovers are still longingly entwined. An invisible hand offers flowers to a beautiful woman. She looks at them with a hard, slightly cold eye. Only the mask remains unmoved…At this point I woke up. I looked at my watch: only 3:30 in the morning. What is there to say at three o'clock in the morning? I look through the window. I cannot see the sun yet and my Teddy is still fast asleep; each white hair of his beard vibrates in my heart. If I could I would wrap him in a halo and grant him eternal life. (That would be a curse!)

And I am conveying to you, my friend, all the chatter my brain contains. You are my soul mate, the woman I love most, because it is my destiny and I cannot change things set in another time, in our previous lives, when we didn't yet know we'd have one soul in two separate bodies. Not the soul of identical twins, but of two strange and different worlds that meet and part and yet remain intertwined, even if harmony is not what it used to be. Do not dare laugh at what I wrote here, even if you do not know about the two worlds. And so, my Ora, listen to me, read the words I have gathered for you...These are the precious memories of a life we once lived out together in the bloom of our days. I have kept them in the envelop of my heart and have taken them out to share them now with you, my friend, my soul's echo.

I told you it is a crazy sun; Lemon trees consumed burning paths on their way. I am pulled to the center of light in you. In the vortex of consciousness you are a glowing gallop. In the abyss of my youth you are an orchid of the sun.

CHAPTER 2

In The Kibbutz

EARLY MORNING IN BOSTON. SOON TEDDY will get up, acknowledge me and say, as usual: *My one and only love.* But I am not here yet; I am still at my mother's home. In my mind's eye, I see my mother all alone, waking from a night of torment, with aching heart and a brittle soul. I am not there to smile at her, or soothe her. Her image in my mind changes suddenly. I see her lips pursed with the injuries of time. I remember greedily eating the hard-boiled eggs and cheese she prepared with her hands full of love and sorrow; hands covered with brown spots painted by a merciless, malignant sun and relentless, shaming age.

Time drains away, says mother, as her lips tighten even more; every line in her face is as deep as a grave. And I did not even visit my father's grave; the Rocky Hill exists only in my stories.

So rest quietly father; rest in peace. There is nothing left. Only... the anemones bloom, as a perennial breeze plays in the tops of the cypress trees. The scent of lilacs caresses the senses and birds fill the universe with their song, as if nothing has changed since creation.

And in the kibbutz? How are things in the kibbutz? In the kibbutz doors are closed like tight mouths, as a paucity of pioneers creep by, their heads bent, eyes half closed, seeking, asking: Where did creation go? What happened to happiness? Where did the colors go? Where are the children? The silence of Genesis floats around them, embraces, penetrates, and their flesh crawls. Out of the silence a voice: Yes; things are changing.

And my brother? I see him too. I hear his voice like a hollow echo, saying what he always used to say when he saw me:, my beautiful sister.

He too wakes, knowing I am not there to caress his forehead with my hand, a hand that has known distant lands, that lovingly drives away the weariness in his head that has turned gray, like a dusty Eucalyptus tree after a heat wave. I think about him, my brother. I speak to him in my head: Do not allow pain to crush you; yours is a magical soul, a pure soul – you do not always understand. Who does? Life changes, drained of light. Children disappoint and parents die. There is a deep, scorching sorrow in one's heart. Sometimes sorrow wins, sometimes joy; don't let pain crush your soul. Fight to the end! And as I thought of him, a shock of pain filled my whole body. So I sat on the toilet, buried my face in my hands and sobbed without tears...

It is quiet in the room. I think again of my mother, remembering her sitting on a chair. I moved across the room, touched the soft skin of her arm and put my face down into her lap. She patted me on the head, a quick nervous pat, not quite an embrace. A cold woman, I remember thinking, a confused face, ambitious and cold, with nothing to give us children, but cold gifts... I remember thinking, later in my life: If I return home I will be like this, an old red- haired woman without feelings, with nothing to give but making mischief, to dance and disappear, dance and disappear. Wild girl, she used to call me; when will you stop all this nonsense and be like the other children? Look at your father, sitting there, smoking and reading, smoking and reading; never has a good word to say. I remember him looking at her and saying in Yiddish, (they all spoke Yiddish and were sure we didn't understand, and although we never used that language, we did.) in a soft controlled voice, Leave her alone, Stella. Don't you see? She wants your love. Give her some. Calm down now; try to understand her. Yes, she is different, but so are you. Who else here works outside, in the city and only returns on weekends to be with the family? I tell you, she misses you, and she longs for you.

Is this how mothers are? You aren't in Vienna now...

I remember her saying to him: What do you know about children, David? What do you know of my needs? I was convinced that when I came to this country it would all be wonderful, but it was not. Living this communal life is not my style. Everyone gossips about each other constantly. I loved you and married you, but I would not sacrifice my life to the commune. You probably forgot how disappointed you were when

Lani, as you call her, was born. You, wanted a son, and you were the only husband who did not bring flowers when his child was born. How do you think I felt – I was insulted to the core of my being. Go back to your books…. she paused then said, and, anyway you will die soon from all these rotten cigarettes…

I ran out of my parents house as fast as I could, all the way to the almond orchard, buried my face in the calming fragrance of their flowers and tried hard to think about something beautiful or funny, but all I could do was cry. I knew what would happen next between my parents. I did not wish to hear the word Nazi again. Ever…

At this point, I blocked my family out of my mind and with three, fast, crazy pirouettes. I jumped towards the kitchen, caught my foot on the slippery rug, fell, injured my knee, cursed, picked myself off the floor and went, limping a little, to the kitchen to make coffee.

CHAPTER 3

Words fail me. Love.

I OPEN THE DOOR; THE SUN IS STILL IN ITS cradle, but the light is soft, new, blue– a little gray, as if warning me that I am in a foreign country and shouldn't become confused or neglectful; I should learn to open myself to the endless possibilities even if they are dim, translucent, dense like paper shadows: diaphanous and foggy, yet always misleading, fooling, teasing; my eyes are blind to them, dazzled by them. I drink the bitter coffee and return to bed. My Teddy walks into the room and kisses my lips. My love, he whispers longingly, exuding a scent of sleep.

We make love, then, with a wild and passionate strangeness. Later I lie beside him, trying to shut my ears to the news of a crumbling world. I never could understand why Teddy insists on starting his day with the polystyrene sound of a sophisticated device from which voices speak terrifying words: Tonight, three children were murdered… the police…

Why not wake to the sounds of music on a new day, even if it isn't all that bright? Grey clouds cover the sky. It will probably rain today. Rain purifies life, or so say the wise.

For the time being, words fail me. Words that once flowed of their own accord onto a page, from a hand no longer as young or beautiful as it used to be, now with its drying skin, and blue veins – I shouldn't exaggerate, even if my mind is still in the grip of nauseating jet lag and sounds come from familiar worlds where things are inevitably different.

Another threatening night; waking up in boiling sheets that smell of metal, yearning for cool hands to caress my forehead, to soothe, to calm the devastation the night inflicted on me – I am full of holes. I rise and go into the living room where all is clean and tidy. The statues stand in place like soldiers, dreaming in the dark morning light. Birds fly out of your pictures on the walls, pecking and shrieking over a bloodbath. What do they want? What do they mean? Why a bloodbath? It is too early to come to conclusions about such serious matters, Twenty to five in the morning: not exactly the hour for a debate. What are people dreaming about now, I wonder curiously? Probably, transparent monsters of darkness are leaping at them from every corner... Oh, and I had forgotten it was Chanukah that week. I dreamt about angels, each with one white and one blue wing. Angels who kissed me and smiled forgivingly – for you are in America, away from our homeland – and I apologized. I had forgotten today was Chanukah. In another dream I wept for the distant love of a strange little girl who lived in her imagination, of a love buried beneath a green tree on a hill shaded by pines and cypress trees, where a wonderful man had chosen to sleep. Forgive me father, I didn't remember that today is Chanukah. In the dream I caressed my lover Eric's beautiful face and touched his gray eyes with my lips as they stared at me with the memory of love and tears for no reason, from eyes that had become ancient.

CHAPTER 4

Eric

I MENTION ERIC NOW BECAUSE I WISH TO TELL you about Eric and Teddy and me. I shall write it to you in the form of a story so my readers will read it too. Stay with me. Here goes:

For forty years my heart leapt at the sound of his voice. His name was like a summons to all my foolish blood. Now my blood is old; slow and lazy, it courses through my veins. Forty years seems eternal, and yet, when He calls and asks me to meet him, I always say yes. The force of habit clutches at my heart, or, perhaps, it is still a surge of love? But that day, (perhaps just to spite him) I didn't say yes right away; I said that I had to ask Teddy first. Really, he asked, surprised. Why? We both knew that I didn't have to ask Teddy. He knows all about Eric and me and, if he bears a grudge, he keeps it to himself.

My darling Teddy, so worldly and bright, most understanding and so gallant - I wish . . . you to walk by my side so I wouldn't have to travel again this arduous way alone.

That you'll protect me so I wouldn't have to bleed between teeth of concealed traps - even from those who pretend to be my friends. That you never throw unkind words at me: only clasp my hand. Let the warmth of your touch flow inside my heart and fill me with calm…

Eric calls again on Thursday and asks if I am free on Friday; he must see me. He says it's urgent. I love you doll, he says, his voice sonorous and sexy. Oh, well, this I cannot ignore - what woman can? So, yes, I say, imitating Molly Bloom's words, yes, I will, yes.

In the evening, when Teddy and I settle down for light dinner of soup and bread that Teddy made (I am a catastrophe in the kitchen; Teddy is a whiz). Tomorrow I am going to dinner with Eric, I say. Teddy's eyebrows rise. With whom, he asks? With Eric, I bark, soup dripping from my mouth. Teddy's lips pucker into a smile, Oh, with Eric, he nods his head, then asks, when will you be back? He pours himself another glass of wine, his fourth (I count.). Never, I say; then I slide to the floor, feigning a faint. (It is sort of an absurd game between Teddy and I when the atmosphere gets tight. As infantile as my antics are, it always makes him laugh.

Actually, I yearn for Teddy to say, even once; that's enough, there is an end to everything; you are my wife, and a wife should be true to her husband, not run around.

But when Teddy asked me to be his wife, he knew he made a package deal. So I give him a kiss and swear in my heart to avenge myself on both of them one night, when the Milky Way is empty and stunned, empty and stunned as was my heart, deserted by Eric, forty years ago, on that sun-scorched beach in Tel-Aviv to squirm and sizzle in the malignant heat:

SUN STUNNED

Sun- stunned we met, then, on the beach. He looked
at me shyly, and asked, may I? I uttered Of course,
and felt my heart leaping to my finger tips. He
smiled, sat close, not touching, playing mindlessly
with a conch. Listen to the sea, he said, pressing the
conch to my ear. I heard the sea simmering inside my
brain; Beware, Beware!

But that same day his body moved on mine, he cooed
lustful words into my breasts. Under my naked body,
sun-scorched- sand-of-noon, was shifting, twisting,
in a delirious swoon. I was burning, my brain inlaid
with seashell shards, the sea shuddering, whispering,
seething, growling and the wind moaning mercilessly.

Then, he tore his body from mine, standing
up, looking at me from somewhere far
above, murmured, shyly, thanks, and walked away.

I watched his distancing back and saw waves-of-prey
licking his feet, the sea swelling, frothing in a primal
rage, corpses of fish floating on its waves. It roared in
a terrible pain, and the wind moaned mercilessly.

When Eric calls on Friday, his voice fails to stir me and there is no spark in my soul, but I say I'll meet him at the Ritz at seven for dinner. What else can I do? Love of forty years is impossible to smother just like that. I'll pick you up at your home, Eric says. OK, I reply (and scream at myself; if I could I would have slapped my face, because he wins again - he always does, and yet, my heart remains cold. Cold? Then why the tingle in my toes?) And my pulse beats like an engine in my throat and then my other voice, whispers to me: You say you love me; you say you care. Why, then, do you play rough with my feelings? You expose your cruel streak, your low self esteem; it simply isn't fair. You say you're coming, then come, or don't say, as it makes you a liar and it makes me your target.

On Friday, at school, the teachers are agitated, stressed from a most intense week, longing for home - so are the children, and, of course, me too. When I enter my house, I drop my purse on the couch and march straight to the mirror. Mirror, mirror on the wall who is the dumbest of them all? My face stares back at me tight and glossy - (so what if I had a little help with stretching and all?) You're so narcissistic, whispers my other voice, after all: no one has benefited from your beauty; you didn't even train a dog, only yourself. You pester me about my looks: What is my image today...Go away, leave me be, I shriek; I thrust my fingers into my ears and begin to cry. I don't change my clothes, nor take my make-up off. I go to the huge window and sit in my big black chair, smoke a cigarette and gaze into the street - how pretty.

Fall gazes back at me, benevolent but gloomy; the soft maple trees stand bare and ghostly in the pallid air; birds are only a vague memory of something cheerful and soft. I watch the evening shadows shroud the world and try not to think pestering thoughts but the chatter in my brain will not cease, buzzing like millions of wasps, memories of yesteryear, when all was different and my other voice whispers to me: remember… there, among the lemon trees and vineyards, through vivid sunrises and through dew you didn't walk in vain. My face lifted to the sky, basking in the Milky Way...of course I remember. How can I forget? But now I wish to dwell in the silence of the mind, to be shut inside a cask, carefully, peek outside to breathe for a moment the light, to smile at a child and again, dive into the silence of my mind and think, not see, expect nothing, only be; for who am I, except blood and tissues, hair, veins, and rotting cells...

But here the voice disappears, because, suddenly, through my window I see a drunk tottering in the street, his face broken into a million pieces, his hopes forgotten and dead. He sits on the low cement by my gate and with shaking hands tries to light a cigarette; it's too windy. He spits. He curses. He takes a swig from his bottle and begins to stumble, but he steadies himself and doesn't fall.

Teddy cautions me repeatedly not to invite strangers into the house It's too risky, he says; you might get yourself raped. He's aware of my weakness for the unfortunate, the miserable, the homeless... But this is a subject to be explored somewhere else. Teddy himself likes his wine strong and red. Anyway, the drunk walks away and disappears into the evening, carrying with him his shattered image.

A pretty young woman with a poodle on a velvet leash is trotting along the street; her eyes are dreamy and there is a silly smile on her lips. A young man, wearing a turned-around baseball hat, meets her. They laugh, they kiss, the hat falls, the poodle barks, but they pay it no heed. Standing under my window, their bodies adhere, and they are licking each other lustily. Beware of the undertow, I want to scream, love is not what it seems. But they vanish into the fog of delusion.

When Teddy comes home, deep evening has gathered the city into its shadows, the world calmed down. The soft maple trees have become spirits. *My one and only*, Teddy says, and devours me with kisses. I bury my face in the soft nook of his neck and implore him not to let me go out with Him- to keep me at home, where I am safe and warm. but Teddy is deaf to my supplications, because, of course,

I only say it inside my head. I have a slash in my heart - an old, old, wound. If you open my brain you'll see bleeding, lacerated and unhealed scars; but also the old fire that still burns in me - for there isn't enough earth to extinguish it.

Seven o'clock: I wait. The doorbell rings. I don't stir. Teddy glances at me, amused. I shrug my shoulders. Teddy gets up and opens the door, and who do you think is standing there, with a smile as wide as a summer night and eyes as wet as rain, if not my old knight? He looks at Teddy and me and smiles at us quietly. Are you ready doll, he asks gently; then shakes Teddy's hand and says, Hi Ted. How good to see you. Sit down, says Teddy, Would you like a glass of wine? No thanks, he answers. Perhaps some other time.

Bye, says my Teddy, enjoy the evening, and he pats my head, as if I were his daughter, then gives me a hurried kiss. My heart doesn't crumble; it moans, and as I walk to the door, I trip on the rug (like the drunk, remember?) and almost fall - four arms reach out and hold me, but my ears are ringing and I begin to snort. I kick the wall. No one sees, no one knows, because, it isn't me - it's only my ghost. I shoot a murderous look at Teddy, but he merely smiles and pinches my cheek. I am tempted to hit him, but immediately the hushed voice is there to remind me that when I met Teddy...

> He came in the dark took my hand, led me a bride into the light that at first was merely a hesitating flicker, then burst and splashed a wondrous shadow.
>
> We entered - his hand did not leave mine. He breathed my breath, as if he were inside, although I knew I'd return to the dark, I glided into the calm of his hand holding mine.

And so it is, now, Eric and I, going again into the night - so far away from that white burning beach where we first met forty years ago. Eric holds my hand and says for the thousandth and one time,

You're so pretty doll. But I am not as quick as all that; I am still thinking of the drunkard, of Teddy, and of the love-stricken lady. He kisses me and they all fade except Teddy. I love you, He says, his voice, deep, caressing and steady-and suddenly my Teddy disappears too, and my world turns crazy –

> The rest of that evening is peaches and cream, dimmed lights and pink champagne poisoned with dreams, and gray snails on a blood-red platter, slippery and slimy as the gutter.
>
> Murmurs wafting in the smoke-drenched air, and memories of love lurking everywhere, shadow-like, touch on a starlit night. Time is bewitched. I am

glowing, I am flying, but between us a wall of fog lies, and I am hateful; my body weeps.

Flutter of lips in the dark, like the flutter of moths' wings, and from a black man, like lava from a dark mountain, erupt love songs that even God has forgotten.

Suddenly a scorching heat, a whisper, Are you with me, my love? And I know, again the time has come to part. A stony silence fills my heart.

Then, at ten, on the porch of my home, He kisses my lips in a beastly heat, and abandons me, as always (His wife is waiting.). I sit on the steps, bury my face in my hands and slowly return to myself. As I open the door, I see Teddy, still staring at the television as if enchanted, because, naturally, he takes the whole thing completely for granted. Hello, my love, he says, did you enjoy yourself? He isn't joking, but I detect a slight tension in his eyes. I drank a lot of champagne and had a ball. Teddy laughs, his face relaxes. Give us a kiss, my love, eh, he says and slaps his knee. I go to him and sit in his lap and wrap my arms around his neck, while Eric's gentle voice is still vibrating in my head, and the champagne is still buzzing confusion in my consciousness. But do you love me? asks Teddy, as he kisses my eyes. Enough! I've had it for today! So I run to my room, get the old reliable bong out from its secret place, and inhale grass until I am good and stoned. Then I shed my clothes, mumble a curse, and like a worm, squirm into bed, pull the covers over my head, thinking, what a mess; I must stop this or else ... but, what a waste - because I love them both and know that I'll never let go of Teddy or Eric.

CHAPTER 5

Childhood Friends

ALPHA, MY CHILDHOOD LOVE, CAME IN AND said; so honey pie, how are you feeling? She was big and hearty, and filled the room with her body, white hair covering her temples. She sighed, waving a newspaper to dry drops of perspiration and cool her hot forehead. After that she sat and listened, saying nothing, but her eyes were filled with understanding and shining with affection. Love of a youth long gone: blue mornings, birds shrieking, and children playing in fields of ripening wheat, perfume of wild flowers, loads of snails after rain, smooth worms and noisy frogs, as well as creeping turtles and gray mice rushing, and giant spiders suspended from transparent silk webs, and snakes with eyes that never close, nervous chameleons and many other animals. This divine symphony was conducted by the yellow sun of childhood that paints faces, eyes and hair with gold, sprinkling big brown freckles, like round pennies, when coins still had holes in them . . . but all this was a long time ago. Today the sun paints the kibbutz in sadness, pain and insults. My brother still carries the disappointment of that crumbling dream in his heart.

My Alpha is dead now. When I heard of her death, I sat at home for three days and howled like a wolf whose cubs have been eaten. Ah, my Alpha, I mourned! Rest in peace my love, your suffering is at an end, and only my great sorrow accompanies you to the silence we do not know.

> One should be able to cry. You do it in secret. Insulted and estranged you walked heavily inside the fortress of silence you imposed upon yourself.
>
> The doves still chatter on the roof of your house in the mornings and each day paints a fresh wrinkle in the face of the loneliness with which you veiled your days.
>
> Let the tears cool the burns of longing in those that death has devoured. Free your tears from metal; your roar will shatter heavens.
>
> What am I without you? Your voice brings beauty back to me. I still hear the two of us singing Radiant Childhood.
>
> But even then, in the light, loneliness stalked you—
> Also me.

After Alpha left, Dahlia, another childhood friend I loved came in. All dripping with sweat, every pimple on her face a burning beacon, and with a heart pinned to her chest she said; just a small gift, handing me tiny white muslin handkerchiefs I was certain no longer existed in the world. They were certainly not made by Kleenex. She gave me a cassette of music, touching her burning cheek against mine. An odor of spices and perspiration came from her. I couldn't bear it, so I opened the safety pin, and with quivering fingers, took the heart and returned it carefully to her chest, saying; take care of your heart, my precious. And she laughed.

CHAPTER 6

Vienna

YEARS LATER, ON ONE OF MY VISITS, MY mother asked me to take her to Vienna once more. She said she would like to visit her childhood house, her school, if it still exists, to eat Mozart Kugels. Take me to Vienna one more time, she said. I asked Teddy what he thought. He said I should go with her and he would join us in four days. I wasn't sure. We quarreled constantly, but I also knew this might be an important trip – to be alone with my mother for four days. It had never happened before, and I wasn't a little girl any more. I was in my early forties...

Am I pretty, Mother? I asked. You're beautiful, she laughed, and kissed my lips. For a fleeting moment she was young, bright and as full of hopes and dreams as a bride, the way she was years ago, when we were at her birthplace, in Vienna. We were there, just my mother and I, talking and laughing, without need for opiates. We lay on a soft bed covered with a plump, old eiderdown. We even walked arm in arm, just for contact. Touching and feeling each other at every moment – as if taking a break from time – And you, Mother, you were wonderful! All dreams came from you into me. The memories of my childhood, my galloping days, the photograph and the negative…the stranger and the self, you fill me with crumbling sweetness.

I kept devouring Mozart Cakes, unable to stop. I got a terrible stomach-ache. When we came to the cemetery, a world of imposing monuments and headstones, beneath which lay the crumbling, worm-eaten dead, we were unable to find Grandfather's grave. So, we went to the graveyard office where we found a tall, skeletal man with transparent hands. One could see a map of veins and bones through his skin. On his head sprouted a few red hairs and his eyes were yellow and sunken in gray cheeks – Well, after all we were in a cemetery. Mother asked in polite German if he could help her find Schnapps grave

(This was the name of my grandfather, who had lain in the earth for many years and whose skeleton was shining white. Naturally Mother didn't say these words. I said them inside my head).

The man placed a pair of huge glasses with a black metal frame on his nose, growled, frowned, squinted and finally opened up a large book, soon examining the millions of lines and billions of names with great self importance. While waiting, Mother's feet became swollen out of her shoes, but she didn't so much as groan. My belly hurt terribly and I needed to go to the lavatory, but was too shy to ask, even though I was already a big girl. The man just continued moving through the pages, with a long, thin finger that was like a dried sausage that he dipped into a green sponge in yellow water, as disgusting as vomit. Finally he spoke: Aha! Then he said something in German that I didn't understand, but my mother's eyes sparkled and she wasn't grieving. It was as if it wasn't her father at all. I became a little confused, I didn't really understand because when I think about my father, I lose my breath. The cemetery caretaker kept telling my mother things I didn't understand, but she listened attentively and kept repeating: Bitte Sichuan mein Herr, und Danke sehr. (You are welcome sir, and thank you.) Soon we were walking among the graves; it was terribly hot, but my mother's feet didn't hurt and she walked quickly and joyfully, just like she had done when she was a pioneer in Israel. The only thing missing was a blue blouse.

We walked among the graves; there, in straight never-ending lines they were, and under huge trees and many colored flowers. From a naked blue-gray sky a merciless sun seemed to beat down, as buckets of sweat poured out of my body. My unwavering mother however, continued walking among the graves like a soldier marching to war. It took quite some time before we finally found my grandfather's grave, and my heart fell. The tomb was so pitiful I almost started to laugh. Mother apologized, saying there wasn't enough money to find something finer, but it did not matter; I do not care about graves; they are just an illusion… I didn't even visit my father's grave on the kibbutz, up there on the Rocky Hill, under the pines and cypress trees…But, I am repeating myself and straying from the subject –

What is the subject? Oh, yes… graves in Vienna:

Unable to hold nature's demands in anymore, I told my Mother I needed to go to the bathroom. Instantly wide-eyed, she stared at me as if seeing me from a great distance and then, she suddenly laughed a crazy laugh. Not really crazy, yet crazy… For a moment she became a naughty little girl with eyes shining in the sun, even though it was a Nazi sun. She said: Go on! Find yourself a place far away from grandfather's grave… over there! Raising her hand and pointing, her lips were pursed in distaste: Over there, on the other side, where the non-Jews are buried. What? I asked; behind a headstone? Mother just laughed, insisting, no one will ever know. And I thought to myself: Troublemaker! So uncivilized. I know it isn't nice. But quite honestly, no-one seemed to care. No one was there. So off I went and found the largest and most beautiful monument on the non-Jewish side, laughing to myself all the time, I kept remembering an infantile joke about Hershel from Ostropol… but

I am certainly not going to tell that one here. After all as Mother says, There's a limit to everything. The problem is that I was never sure where or what the limit is. Well, never mind. Limits are far too complicated a subject.

I did what I needed to do and then I couldn't find my mother. Everything around me had become weird and spooky. Now I seemed to be walking among those grand graves in the company of Grandfather Schnap, with his black capote and bony hands. I almost spoke to him, badly wanting to know what it was like to be dead, but in the end I realized that everyone has his or her own experience. In any case, who says he would have answered? Nevertheless it was an amusing, indeed very strange, experience. My mother was so very happy, lovely and youthful that I felt I hardly knew her. But she really loved me, even more than loved me... there in Vienna of all places. I'd never seen her like that, didn't know she could be so wonderful. And wherever we went they said, Gr. Gott! (May God greet you!) It was an everyday greeting more often uttered with tight lips and a sour heart, than any other way. I also said Gr. Gott, with zipped lips and clenched teeth and, like a witch, I straightened my back, lifted my head and clicked my heels, like a real Nazi from the war. My mother said, that it wasn't nice behavior, and that I was impossible (people always tell me I'm impossible, I'm used to it), and didn't know how to behave, but nothing helped. I'd had enough of those nauseating Nazis, so I made fun of them wherever we went. Oh, these were the happiest days I remember. I wished it had lasted forever. Four days later, Teddy joined us and the harmony was disrupted.

CHAPTER 7

Stay a While

BACK IN BOSTON, IT IS EARLY MORNING. I GO to make coffee. A cloudy morning fills the kitchen window. It's very quiet around me, as if all the people have died and the world is mine alone. Within the rising of the sun, I see all of you, my dearest friends, passing through my life, pausing for a moment, smiling, caressing, promising and then vanishing. Then you reappear, follow me for a while before disappearing again, as if I were a pathway or a door. You enter my world, but you do not stay. Even so, I am inside you as you are inside me. Morning fades away and you forget that I'm here. This is my life still clinging to you – and letting go. I tell myself: There is not much time left. You pass beneath the columns of my spirit, come up, stay a moment, hold me.

Again I gaze through my window at the sky, of a pearly color now. Teddy is still asleep. Yesterday evening he went for a radio interview concerning his jazz CD. He was nervous and not particularly friendly. As for me, I was still so self-absorbed I forgot to ask how it went, what he did and what he said. My spirit was dead to the world when he returned. From his perspective, he very much wanted to love and be close, to make love, but I couldn't be with him. Leaving Teddy alone with his experience and disappointment, again I'd folded myself away deep inside in a place of utter solitude, letting sleep gather me up.

CHAPTER 8

Stars

NOT ONCE, DURING MY STAY IN HER HOME on the kibbutz did my mother mention The Rocky Hill, which was the cemetery for members of the kibbutz, before things changed; my father is buried there, too. She never asked to visit the grave of my amputee father (due to an accident), who was eventually devoured by cancer. His grave was set high up there. So rest quietly, Father, there beneath the cypress on the Rocky Hill, rest calmly – soon, now, I'll be there with you, father. Father!

I remember him looking at me with half-closed gray eyes, such sad eyes. I saw death reflected in the pupils of his eyes, crawling like a snake between the lines in his forehead and his cheeks. And I asked myself: what was his life like? What did he want? Did he ever love? ...Seated at our table, I see him shrouded in cigarette smoke, his sad, beloved eyes staring towards the distance, enveloped in dream clouds, as though he were waiting for the ultimate silence. What thought disturbs him? What desire? Why the sadness? But I knew: Oh; in those camps his entire family was gassed by the Nazis, leaving him with an oozing void in his heart, an oppressive void, a shouting void. He couldn't find a refuge inside himself. He died, my beloved man. There is no solace for me. Only sadness. Only silence.

I couldn't bring myself to visit his grave, since that day, when I stood stone-like, dry eyed (dressed in the denim-dress, he liked so much) next to a black hole in which they put the man. There on the Rocky Hill among cypress and pines trees (perhaps now he will have peace and love) they covered the man with the broken heart and amputated hand with black earth: the man I love more than anyone, my father, who has gone from my life.

I remember in particular one day in the kibbutz: All ten of us would lie on the lawn in front of the dining room after dinner, stretched out on the slightly wet grass: children from my group, usually on Fridays, our heads resting on someone's thigh or chest or belly; we probably looked like a heap of moving critters. We sang the songs of our country, looking up at the deep blue sky, where every star seemed instilled with the pure light of magic.

That particular, evening I was in one of my dreamlands, my head on Rami's belly, (Rami was my closest friend from our group of ten) his head on Dahlia's thigh. I had not joined the singing; I was staring at the stars, trying to understand their secrets. Suddenly my vision concentrated on a particular star, which seemed smaller than others, and in front of my disbelieving eyes, this star began to move towards me, or was it my imagination? To this day I have not made sense of that phenomenon. Anyway, I waited; my body became still, soft and open; the star kept approaching; its light filled me with utter calm, complete silence.

Hey, Lani, what's going on with you? asked Rami. You seem to be glowing all over, your entire face shines like a star. He looked at me curiously, perhaps a little alarmed. Rami, I blurted without thinking, I just swallowed a star. He smiled; you and your fantasies; no one swallows stars; stop being so weird; every day you invent something spooky. Now it is a star you are involved with; the other day it was... he paused. What was it? I seem to have forgotten, it was something about oneness, you had the idea that the entire world is one and that all things in the world are interwoven with one another.

I stopped him. I said, I read this book, Meditations, by Marcus Aurelius; I stole it from my father's library. I didn't understand all of it, but this idea stuck with me; it made so much sense. I tell things as I see them, as they come to me. Now, let's join the singing. You invent the strangest stories, mainly at night, said Rami, shaking his head. Sometimes you scare us all; like that story about the snake and the woman in the woods. This weirdness is deep in my being,

I am the way I am, Rami. I am not able to be different. So let me be, now.

I was about twelve years old then. I jumped to my feet and ran to my parents little apartment to say hello to my father. Mother was not home. She only came home at weekends, if at all. As I entered, I saw my father sitting at the table in the living room, wrapped in a cloud of cigarette smoke; his somber, beloved eyes gazing outward as if waiting for the final stillness. What was he thinking? What did he want? Why was he so sad?

Shalom father, I chirped, as I entered the room and began, as was my habit, to jump and dance around the room, circling my father's chair. He encouraged me: Dance Lani, dance, he would say. I would continue to dance and he would melt. Suddenly I heard him say, Lani, what is it with you, my little girl? What did you do today? He gave me a quick puff of his cigarette. What is it, Lani, you seem so restless? Daddy, I began, then stopped and looked at his face searchingly. Oh, come on Lani, what's on your mind?

I don't think I am from here! I remember announcing a little defiantly. My father's face assumed an interested, rather amused, expression. So, where do you come from? He looked at me curiously. When I didn't answer, he said, What makes you think you are from a different place, Lani; want to talk about it? I am not sure I want to talk about it, I said, feeling a little confused and terribly misplaced. I looked at him thinking: I love this man, my father. I can trust him.

I came from a star, I looked daringly into his eyes, waiting for the words; *don't be silly, Lani,* which never came. He just looked at me and waited, lighting one cigarette with another.

I am different from everyone else… I stopped talking and began to dance again; this time I was practicing my ballet. I pirouetted around the room on the tips of my toes and hummed some music to myself. My ballet teacher said to me the other day that she believes I shall be a great ballerina if I practice all the time (And I did).

Father sat in silence and watched me through the clouds of smoke surrounding him. He didn't stop me. I turned to him and said; I look different. I act differently. I even think differently from all my friends. I know they think I am weird; they don't say so, but I know. It feels peculiar to be estranged from your own friends. Then, something happened; I knew I came from somewhere else, a star. I came from a star. I had to take a breath, I was talking too fast. My father caressed my head and said softly, my Lani from the stars. You are my Lani from the stars. And the name stayed with me from that day on. I was only twelve years old. My father paused, smiled, and then his eyes grew serious. Life is difficult for you. I lowered my eyes. Don't be sad, my Lani, he said softly, everything has a purpose. I promise you, one day you will not feel weird; the time will come and you will find yourself. Now you must control yourself. You cannot just disappear for hours and cause everyone to search for you. Where do you disappear to, and why?

Oh, Dad, I said, you know where I go… He nodded his head; yes, I know. I even followed you a few times. Don't you think, you should go to school? You must learn all that…" NO, I shouted in his face, school is boring, the teachers are stupid. I do not listen to what they say. I can read it in the books, sitting on the Kissing Stone in the woods, breathing, listening to bird songs. Butterflies fan my cheeks. Every now and then I see a black snake slithering among the leaves. Oh, dad, it is so beautiful and I feel so happy. Isn't it the reason you taught me to read when I was three years old? Please don't get mad at me now – I know you are not, because when I was a little child I heard my mother say to you, David, David, what shall we do with the child (I hated it when she called me *The Child.*); I am very worried (I didn't understand, then, what was she worried about). Anyway she isn't important. She is never here, and when she is she is mostly angry with me. She told me that when I was born, she was sure that they changed babies and gave her the wrong girl, who was born at the same time. Is it true Daddy? Is it true? He lit another cigarette, Come little Lani, have another puff. I understood then that he didn't wish to talk about my mother; his eyes became even sadder. I love you so much my one and only Daddy. Tears were stinging my eyes. We were quiet for a while, and then he said: Dance Lani, Dance. I danced and he cried.

Suddenly I remember myself, a little girl of four, standing next to my father, while he read a book without even glancing at me… as I prayed to the God of the Jews for a miracle. I just needed a small one for me, so that my father would see me, pick me up in his arms, hug me and whisper, My child, kissing my lips, that he would caress my hair and touch my cheeks and forehead with the tips of his fingers. God, however, didn't hear my prayer, and my Father didn't see me or collect me to his arms; he just read that terrible book. He visited only years later when he was no longer alive. At the very core of the night he came; he uttered not a word, only stood there, head bowed, his body exuding malignant sorrow. The next night he came again. I was waiting for him, awake, my mind quivering and tense; Is it you. Say, is it you? (But of course I knew who he was). He lifted his eyes, a faint smile swept over his mouth, he looked at me for a long time, with beloved, pained eyes and he stretched shadow-arms to me. I arose from the bed, floated toward him on the dusky-dark air, but he melted away. A faint scent of tobacco and rosemary lingered on the air. I remained alone in the night, aching for the solace of the light.

One night after the moon came out, I walked again to the distant almond orchard that stood in a dream of white blossom. I hid there for many hours and no one knew where I was. When they finally found me, my face was buried in almond blossom. Yet, I was never harshly treated. My father was an enlightened person. Children, he would say, should be treated gently, and lovingly educated with a great deal of patience and understanding. So, you tell me, isn't that a joke? I wished to be beaten hard and painfully, so that the other pain might go away. My mother was hardly ever there, and mostly a shadow on the cracked walls of the room.

CHAPTER 9

Muse

IN A FEW MOMENTS TEDDY WILL COME TO MY room and gather me to his heart, the smell of sleep escaping from his body; and he'll whisper into my neck, My one and only love, but maybe not, perhaps he'll forget. Forget me, just like my father who went to join the dead. Teddy comes to my room and into my bed with a sigh – he doesn't say love, doesn't make love, just asks: I ask, what? Time to get up already…? How long have I been awake? Moments of grace are so rare; they steal into our lives very sparingly. I send him off to take a shower, then stand up and shout: Good morning world! The neighbor's dog barks in reply. (Tomorrow I will sunbathe again in the moonlight.)

The days gallop by like a familiar dream; the nights are full of stars and images. My eyes are wide open in the darkness. Winter fell upon us without warning and I am still not ready. The window in my room is full of gray light. Absorbed into my eyes, it is stealthily paralyzing my fingertips, and the Muse has also turned her back on me. I am waiting, waiting for her to return to wrap me in her smile, but she tarries, taking her time. There is no urging or cajoling her, neither kindly nor unkindly. You could not win her over with a wink, for she is much like a byzantine woman: Please help me, Muse!

> Day after day I fear it's the last poem, but I will not wither and dry up even if that is the outrageous truth. Every morning I will sit down to the naked page and the turmoil of my thoughts.

> Who are you, Muse, if not a friend to the flight of imagination?

> Do what you do so well, be a friend! Don't despair or fix your stern eyes upon me.

> Remember, I'm yours by virtue of love. Don't mock me or turn your crooked back on me. Soften your fickle heart; be generous. I'll sing my best poems to you; I'll write poems of peace and you will bless me with dreams, rhymes and fruitfulness.

Even Charlie my wonderful computer stands here in plastic dreaminess, ashamed. I covered him so he wouldn't look at me with pleading accusation in his eyes – paralyzed and mortified. All my heroes, creations, and inner voices completely disappear, while my stories and letters collect dust in a drawer; I look through inverted binoculars and you are far away, Ora. But at times I see you with amazing clarity, painting up there on the roof of your home in

Tel-Aviv, while I embroider and chatter away; harmony reigns between us. It is a more important harmony than the dubious love between a man and a woman, as everything becomes black and white again. I even criticize myself: You fool, that's life; nothing exists forever. A very poor comfort, for things overturn and change; everything becomes confused inside; I so want to believe, but don't. I know that to believe is actually not to know, and within our inner self (soul?) there is a part that is threatened, nauseated. Contradiction is what you'd call it and there is silence. The silence of the Lamb - the Jewish people who came from Europe after the second war and never mentioned the Holocaust. I used to wonder if they are ashamed they didn't fight, or is it too horrible for them to talk about it? We called them the silent people. Expectation turns to disappointment, love is an illusion reflected in a mirror and every genuine smile is an unexpected gift that falls randomly from the wings of angels who dwell in a farthermost galaxy. Maybe you and I shall be together again, I hope in Tel-Aviv...for our memories are transparent, distinct, and pure, filled with joy and light. Perhaps your mother and my father, (both departed) meet among the flowers and the doves in heaven and play at exchanging worms. Oh, why do I let life mess with my soul? Do tell me, my dear, after all you know me so well, or so you say.

Yesterday, I said to Teddy: Say something funny. I like holding your foot, he answered, as he laughed like a lunatic, and I echoed him like a barrel full of monkeys. My poor Teddy, he hovers around so helplessly, with his eyes sadder than usual. In his heart of hearts he probably wishes me dead so he can live in peace and quiet. Poor, Teddy… (What if he really does?)

CHAPTER 10

Piter's Restaurant

THIS MORNING I INVITED MYSELF TO BREAK-fast at a local café. Do you remember that scruffy restaurant? Piters. We had a little fight there that almost finished off our love. It was terrible, but we made it... Let's get back to the restaurant; The food was terrible, but I blended in well with the human landscape of the wretched, the oppressed and those who sleep in barrels (like in Beckett's play), the horny, the stunned, the old, those with empty eyes who have nothing to live for and don't know if they are alive or dead. I felt completely at home; (Kafka's home.).

It is a lovely day outside. There is even a sun that tricks the city with its hazardous beauty. I went back home and cried a little. I'm full of self-pity today for some reason. After all, I do have an unhappy husband, as well as suitors (girl-friends – not so much) , but things aren't too bad – I even have books and someone who loves me enormously. So, as you say, what else does a person need? Now I'm going to stand on my head, it always restores my sanity. Write me a nice letter from our country.

Again I look like a scarecrow, frightening the birds. I just can't continue anymore, so badly wanting to be an orphan. Oh, the guilt, the guilt! Now, I look out of my window at the sky, clear as white wine, as if there were no rape, murder, or bloody wars beneath it. But why is the sky to blame? Something has to be blamed, right? Do you remember the man in the wall... you can always blame the man in the wall. Oops! I almost started to write again about the train I missed; but no, I'm not going to torture you again with my silly whims because I do love you, Ora, and that is the truth. What truth? Is there such a thing?

CHAPTER 11

Letters

LET ME TELL YOU SOMETHING THAT HAPPENED to me with a glamorous woman who knows everything, unquestionably. We were talking about a very dangerous subject, the meaning of truth. Maggie announced that there is good and bad in the world, but nothing in between. I thought to myself – know-it-all. I didn't argue with her, just swallowed and sniffed, as she glared at me and asked: Don't you agree? I answered, Who me?

I have no opinion about such complexities, but then she insisted, Don't bullshit me, okay? And I just told her; so don't talk nonsense… Finally, we dropped the dangerous subject and stayed friends for the time being, despite our disagreement. That's a serious achievement, especially for me. The next day I received the jewel of a letter from her. Here is the letter as I received it:

A LETTER FROM MAGGIE.

…All night I thought (writes Maggie): my poor Lani, it's hopeless, you will never understand that your mouth is just a muscle! Involuntary! Nothing can control it; not confidence in yourself, or certain values that dictate what to say, when! Your mouth issues words, appropriate or not, out of place, or not. Tell the truth; tell a secret, a lie, randomly, without any control! And I ask myself why you react so strongly to this terrible fault in your friend. For forty years now you have quietly, smilingly, put up with her. When I asked you not to tell anyone in Israel that I was separating from my husband because it was a secret, because I wanted to protect my family in Israel, you blurted it out the minute you got there, and then wallowed in tiny vulgar lies – we let go of it because little

Lani was turning 40. For a year I forgave insults, inattention, complaints and anger; Maggie and Lani always knew how to take care of little Lani, because somehow Lani didn't have a clue, always lacked control. Lack! Lack! Lack! Now what's happened to Maggie? She can't stand up to one big flaw of a friend! This is the reason why I'm so mad again! Your lack of control over your mouth, your lack of sense is incredible to me. I'm sick and tired of it! No, don't answer please. Any words you might have, for better or for worse, poison me! How much time have you willingly spent on huge quantities of good and bad bullshit. Whatever! You open and close those beautiful lips of yours, let out air, and you haven't the faintest idea of what exactly you're saying! How many times have you heard me say we shouldn't talk to friends' kids about their parents! And you heard, but you never listened, because your greatest fault is this inability to really listen. You know the words but you haven't the slightest idea of what attention means. It's appalling. A disability! So this lack, lack, and lack I am only now digesting. This lack cuts into my heart like a knife because I'm actually very slow. I knew but didn't want to know how much you've worn me out, and alarmed, hurt and angered me as well, which only goes to show how important you were to me, and how much you took me for granted, how much I've put up with all these years, the terrible things you've said and done, or haven't done. You've always talked so much about your love for me! You loved me because I made you feel good, and let you verbally abuse me. And now the machine has broken down and I don't have the strength to give you what I always used to give you: attention, a one-sided dialog.

A RESPONSE FROM LANI TO MAGGIE

(which was never sent):

Maggie, you deserve a prize for your last letter and for the quality of your writing too, but most of all for your self-awareness camouflaged as always, as a cry to the heavens. What you write about me is exactly what I think about you, and not only today, but have done for a long time now. My thoughts about you are precisely what you write, just that

I have a few more things to say about you that have to do with your huge lies, phony behavior, appalling self-ishness, your unrepentant delays, last minute cancelations, coarse language in relation to your friends, such as: 'That cow Nora' or Dahlia, who'd have laid down her life for you. I remember you calling her a 'doormat' and more, even saying 'that Fool Ariel.' She succeeded where you failed. There was even your contempt for my friends Tamara, Naomi, and Mina, but most of all it was how you almost managed to destroy the wonderful relationship I had with Ora, for which I will never forgive you. And so much more – you were almost drooling with pleasure at putting all of them down. You are filled with hidden corners, sinister secrets, and bitter insinuations. I did get angry sometimes, but when I realized that it's an illness, that there's even a medical term for it, I told myself: We'll forgive Maggie. She has other qualities too. I cast you out from my heart a long time ago. It was a long, slow process, almost like a death; it took a year I think, maybe even longer. I always knew it would end badly, for you aren't capable of hearing anything that isn't complimentary to you, and you aren't capable of confrontation without a verbal explosion and screaming, no matter where you are – in a restaurant, or on the phone or writing a letter. With all your grandiose behavior, you don't understand that being humble is the hardest of all! So now I repeat what I wrote. Switch the names around in your letter and you'll realize that you were actually writing about yourself. I hope this will help you to understand that you cannot abuse people. Ultimately it will all come back to you like a boomerang – You ought to learn about yourself from your letter, not about me. I already know who I am. A long time ago I told you that a part of me feels as if disabled, lacking and I will always be that way. It's who I am, but this has nothing to do with what you say here and only a small part of your total disability. You are a very sick woman who does not have a clue about yourself. Our relationship has long been a ritual obligation. So do a little exercise and switch the names round in your letter and maybe, just maybe, you'll understand that you're talking about yourself. (Or as an afterthought, perhaps about your cruel mother.) I'm not going to respond to what you say about children, even though I have a very clear opinion about that, but since I won't be sending you this letter anyway, I can only say that you have destroyed your children. Neither of them can cope with life, and now you're picking on your grandchildren. Let me tell you a little secret; for the past year or so, every time we met I took Xanax beforehand, because the poison coming out of your mouth put me into a terrible state of anxiety. Words of love are nothing to sneer at. I loved you with all my heart, but not because you were nice or made me feel good. I was always afraid of you… but that's for a profound talk…Sincerely, Lani.

There are other ways to say it – as Rilke wrote: 'masks, banalities'. So what? Life is mostly banal and moments of transcendence have faces that are not quick to emerge; there are people who do not have a face at all – merely heads without a face. The main thing is to live; to be. Holding on is the main thing. That's what those who know have to say. An example… This morning I saw a blind man waiting to cross the street. I touched his arm and asked, Can I help you? He almost hit me with his cane, Go away, he hissed, Go away bitch! He shook his fist at the sky and shouted: The pit…the pit!

What pit? I asked, but he continued to shake his cane in the air and his fist at the sky. I covered my face with my hands and when I raised my head the blind man had disappeared. I realized he was from Neverland and as always I was alone, so I went home, wrapped myself in a blanket, sat on the stairs of my house, and watched the sparrows, tiny unpretentious creatures, and I wondered how a bird feels; but I couldn't even begin to understand. Maybe a mistake made in Creation; perhaps birds were created out of His love, and Man out of His hatred.

CHAPTER 12

Apple. Face Lift

ONE OF THOSE MYSTERIOUS NIGHTS, WHEN the air is white and liquid, and a kaleidoscope of images whirls around. A dark moon smirked and sneered, a moon without comfort or beauty, a loveless moon… a jealous moon in a white night thick with doubts and elusive half dreams, which leave my insides hollow and my brain tacky. Do you know about such nights? Yes, of course you do. It was you who told me about face-lifts: blue, green, yellow: the cutting of the flesh as if being slaughtered, but without fear. The pain is transcended by the thought: tomorrow I'll be beautiful again. Death. There must be no fear in death. Life is only a metaphor, you said, or did I say that? No matter. But if that is so why cut the face? Why change what is preordained? Why tamper with nature? There is no nature, only a face… a face swollen like a full moon… a painted moon, or maybe a dream. It might all be a dream; the knife, the blood, pain; all a dream. You wake up one morning, look in the mirror and gasp: Me? Is this me? Yes, it's me inside. Outside a stranger glares into my eyes; a faulty reflection, a distorted image. When did the years pass? So, you are cut and stretched and you change. Anticipation, exquisite agony. Madness. New you? New me...? Youth captured once more? Eternity? Well, that's a good question. The Bushmen of the Kalahari Desert say there is a dream always dreaming us.

You my friend went to Germany for a face-lift operation. What a trip you must have had with a train ride through German landscape. Were you thinking of Nazis and gas chambers? Being Jewish is forever. No. It is not right even if you think of it from your other side, or if you peel away the pretense that you are right, not even if you insist: I don't know, I don't understand. I know I am only alive and all of it belongs to the distant past anyway. Even then it isn't right for you or for me or for anyone of our kind to go on a train in a German land. Were you alienated? Didn't you belong? You belong to all and everywhere, but no one wants to remember because if one remembers one has to care. So we cut even deeper and the blue turns purple, the green yellow, they all merge and become one. One ancient tree; a tree of Eden: old, gnarled, wrinkled, cracked and twisted; but on its top are a few green leaves still fluttering in the wind as if to say: We are still here. Look! Life, Love and Space... or perhaps they are simply just a place?

St. John said that in the beginning was the Word. Do you recognize this? One word, but did anyone ever find the right word? Maybe you will and maybe you won't. I might, but I know I cannot. What's in a name? asked distraught Juliet of love-stricken Romeo. Everything? Nothing? Just a word? But oh, if I only could find the right word, then the white night will be the right night after all.

A habit, a strange habit, or a thirst for knowledge? I wake up about two o'clock in the morning and feel a craving. A sort of restlessness descends upon me. It is a hunger, a craving, my body tingles with longing. Reflecting on the feelings I discover, of all things it is an apple I crave. All I want is an apple. Wanting to smile at my foolishness, my mouth seems frozen, so I get out of bed and tiptoe to the kitchen. The floor creaks, but there is no fear that Teddy will wake up. My love and husband Teddy, has become deaf and blind through modern devices – eyeshades and ear-plugs, but then again why hear dogs bark in the night? A smart man my Teddy is and the one I tenderly love. I sneak the apple to bed with me, lie on my back and squeeze the apple between my hands. The fruit fragrance drifts across my face and soothes my screaming nerves before I proceed to eat, as if it is the last apple I shall ever eat. Delicious… The night is not white any longer. I have a friend inside me: an apple . . . Words pour out of me. My fingers spell what my mouth dares not say: Am I mad? Is Zeus my God? or

Satan? Did I build a golden calf? Will I gouge out a horses' eyes? Truth is missing from our sight. We chose knowledge instead. We are afraid to dwell inside. Introspection is amiss: "Do I dare to eat a peach?" Indeed! Indeed! Poor T. S. Eliot, he should have had a face lift, but would that have been it? "That is not it at all," said Mr. Eliot. But if that is not it, then what is? This is not funny. It is strange; I feel so strange.

Today after school I felt dizzy with frustration and frenzy, so I went to the executioner, now called a Beauty Designer, and had my hair cut almost to the scalp. Finally returning home, I was feeling even more weird and wacky, and looking in the mirror my ears stuck out like one of those creatures from the ridiculous movie cartoons, Loony Tunes. My face looked white and naked; my nerves were spattered in patterns over the gossamer screen of the indifferent glass, and my wrinkles were dancing in frenzied celebration. Oh, if mirrors only had a heart! Suddenly the image of Van Gogh's mutilated face zapped my mind. I quickly found a needle and pierced one earlobe, then the other. They didn't bleed or hurt, but I still didn't feel any better... a bath, perhaps? What a clever thought! The water in the tub was scalding hot, but no relief was found there either. I don't think that I'll have a face-lift after all. Get old gracefully? Hurray! What a luxurious stupidity. I'll only get old – grace belongs to elephants and children.

Hot flushes… a wet fever… Absurd! Absurd! Of course, it's only menopause. I really feel terrific, so why the pain? I hear God's answer: I do not know.

FACE-LIFT

He opens the door wide offers her a mustached smile
and utters in an oily voice; You're so beautiful.

The wrinkles on her face deepen, her eyes sink in
their sockets. The skin of her neck crumples, the
spots on her hands darken.

He sits in the black leather chair; She perches on
the royal blue couch; In one hand he holds a glass of
white wine; she clutches a tiny mirror to her chest.

Between his lips trembles a cigarette. She stares at
the brown spots on her naked arm (the oil paintings
on his walls are terrific). He laughs, he roars; he
continues to seduce.

Words, words, words, pecking at her like ravens'
shrieks. And though he is her friend of many years,
she does not believe him because his eyes are dead,
his face opaque.

His fingers shake— the wine crumbles his brain. And
she, she only sees how with the downing of each
young morn her beauty drowns into the depth of the
looking glass.

CHAPTER 13

Desert

I WOKE UP TO BIRD SONG. LOOKING OUT THE window I saw a sky bursting with delight and when I saw your letter I was filled with joy. Teddy flew to Paris and Barcelona, and the first night on my own was sublime (a Xanax or two – so what?) Everything around me was quiet in a world of souls, and for some reason you walked into the wilderness, into an ancient silence filled with vanishing voices, spaces rumoring a soothing heat wave and rolling infinity. I remember walking in the desert when I was serving in the army. I walked alone. The night was perfect, the desert waiting - everything in place - beckons to me, silent, pulling me like a magnet toward its secrets. The desert haunted me. Although the moon was only crescent-shaped, the night was intense like a white night, as bright as day, yet much softer. You know, one of those nights when the Milky Way flows all around you and you feel as if you were floating inside it touching the stars with the tip of your fingers. The desert. So pure. I imagined all this living as the same strange experience for you. The city is prose, the desert poetry. How I envy you, dearest Ora. Don't you know that real letters aren't what we plan to write? When we re-read them we are curious, wondering, sometimes startled. These are the true words; giving the hand freedom to write from the subconscious. There is no better way to understand what is happening in that astonishing dwelling place for the secrets of spirit and soul. You and I – where do we belong? We write love letters not even speaking on the telephone. We don't seem to have the need; what is there left to say? We'll coat our words in marzipan, conceal expressions in mountains of smoke; gazing into each other's eyes is sadly impossible. Giving each other a bear-hug is also impracticable. Our treasure is truly our own and our truth is written gradually in letters and not by chance. This is an issue that lies in distinctions between the rational external world and the emotional internal world. You write that you find the creation of environmental and landscape sculptures nauseating. Differing, I find it marvelous – it wasn't for nothing I wrote about it in one of my last poems; LOVE.

And yet, even though it is still cold and murky outside, the wind is howling – Never mind, there are more important things than the weather, like our talk on the phone Saturday; It was a delightful experience for me and I loved you so much, Love. What is love? Is it just a burnt-out word, or does it have some meaning? It knows. It is still; shines and instills yearning, for it does have the power to change lives – sometimes for the better, often for the worse. When good, it is wonderful, when bad - terrible. Love is a frightening word. Yet sometimes a person surpasses himself and, at the sight of a flower in bloom, two people might exchange a glance of wonder as pleasurable as any kiss. Just a look, a sigh, sudden tears, pain momentarily forgotten; sadness disappears as that space is taken over by love, which is always waiting its turn, a little shy, depressed, hesitant, but never gives up, waiting with infinite patience for that extraordinary moment; when a man makes room in his soul, love is swift to steal in, if only for a while.

Oh yes, I dreamed the other night that I had an affair with Yehudi Menuhin. I immediately realized that the dream came to remind me that there is wonderful music in the world and that not every voice comes from Dante's Inferno. There are also pure voices and the eyes of sculptures that express more than human eyes – even if you cut yourself, the wound will ultimately heal. {What an inappropriate metaphor!} And myself? Again I am distant, looking at you, Ora, through reverse binoculars, and you are so tiny, a fairy story woman, and perhaps this is one big mistake, and when I wake I will see Teddy's sad eyes looking at me with a familiar kind of alienation. Another time, another person, and my heart contracts. It is very hard for him to get used to a strange body and he rages at his body and at mine, while writhing on my belly with neither lust nor sensation, and I am insulted and overcome, overcome and insulted.

No, I cannot go through all this, not even at this point in time, even if it is important, even to get beyond the stench. I will stay here with my ironic fate.

When I was born, I sucked at the breasts of a stranger. So what is the question? For example: Why haven't I heard a word from Eric? What is the point of distant love? And again words unspoken, feelings unexpressed, tears unshed, and a temporarily required joy hidden in the tissues. A desire to know what comes before knowing wakens in me and I realize that there is nothing before knowing, and a terrible frustration rises in me and I think of the desert and everything that came before knowing, or if there was anything at all. Existing houses have been destroyed; they collapsed: gaping windows, eyes full of resentment, and the dream of creation and enduring love in an uncomprehending heart:

What does your brother have against me? says Mother. He's my child after all. Come with me mother. We shall go to the desert and count the grains of sand, I say, and fall asleep. Will I wake up tomorrow?

CHAPTER 14

Marta

AND NOW, SINCE WE'RE TALKING ABOUT KIB-
butzim, I'll tell you a story about the kibbutz, or more
accurately, about a certain family I was very close to. Listen
well, friends, and please don't get too upset, even if it breaks
your heart.

Here it is –

All that night, the rain fell thick and insistent. All that
night, Marta was deep into her reveries; the voices hum-
ming far and near, high and low; the visions clear and sharp.
Others as pale as banks of fog. Marta's eyes are closed, but
she is not asleep. She is afraid to sleep. Devoured by cancer,
drowning in morphine, she lies in her bed under the window, listening to the rain, holding her breath, postponing
the pain each breath costs. The rain stops at dawn. She sees
the sunrise in her mind's eye. A red sun bursts forth from
within rain-saturated clouds. Large drops of water glisten-
ing boldly on the branches of the cypress trees, balancing
for a moment, then falling, disappearing into the cracks of
the parched earth.

Her pain is dim and distant. Her imagination hovers in the kibbutz, in the world. She is digging deep into the archives of memories, sunk into the world of images. Now she sees the teacher, Dahlia, meet with her friend, Anna, near the Children's House. Thank God it rained, Anna says. I was getting worried. Another drought would have been a disaster. I must hurry, Dahlia says. The children are all over the place, getting filthy, looking for snails and earthworms. And Marta sees Anna smile, and smoothes a bunch of white hair from her forehead with a calm hand. Relax, Dahlia, she says. The children will get wet anyway. Besides, it's good for them. You mustn't worry so much. You already have an ulcer. Look! Such a beautiful day. It'll probably rain again this afternoon. But Dahlia puckers her forehead, narrows her eyes, sighs, and says, Anna, you always know everything. And she adds quickly, see you, and they disappear. Now she imagines Ezra, her husband, on his way to the sheep pen, meeting with Eli, the kibbutz mechanic. A beautiful day, Ezra. Did you hear the deluge last night? she hears Eli say to her husband. What do you think? Will it be a good year? We live and hope, Ezra mutters. Lots of grass for the sheep. What do you say, Ezra? Yah. Ezra allows himself to be cajoled into a stingy smile. Lots of good grass for the sheep this year.

How is Marta this morning? Eli asks. With her mind's eye, Marta watches her husband, trying not to miss a word.

What will he say? But Ezra only shakes his head. Are those tears in his eyes? She isn't certain. Her imagination follows her distancing husband, his hands deep inside his pockets, his shoulders hunched. Ezra, straighten up, she says out loud, startled by her own voice.

Near the dining hall, she sees children playing boisterously, chasing one another, sloshing in the mud, jumping into puddles of water, shrieking with laughter as they gather little rain critters, which had appeared overnight. Dahlia, the teacher, is beside herself. Little Micha, she admonishes, you'll catch cold! Nati, look how wet and muddy you are. Daphna, let go of those worms. You're crushing the poor creatures. Nati, Nati, look, I've got five snails, she hears Little Micha say to Nati. Little Micha, look at the rainbow! cries Nati.

Nati, my little angel, Marta whispers. She places her hands on her heart and, with a great effort, opens her eyes. The shutters are closed, the curtains drawn. She does not want the sun. Light is of no use to her. She lies inert, as if dead. Only her eyes, two green dots in a gray face, shine feverishly in the dimness of her room. Where is Ezra? she mutters, then smiles. She knows where he is: in the fields tending the sheep, dreaming of young women with heavy breasts. How she misses the green pastures, the endless wide meadows. The smell of the earth used to intoxicate her, fill her with a sensuous pleasure. The land is in her soul, in her body, her decaying body.

How lucky Ezra is, her silly husband, who like all other men loses his head to the sight of big breasts and full thighs. The thought brings a spasm of familiar pain in the pit of her gut. She never quite understood why she had married him in the first place, except that they were both young and enkindled by a dream. And he had been so handsome. In the little Polish town where they were born, he had been a teacher, respected and admired by everyone. They met one summer at a Zionist group meeting, and he fell in love with her, or so he said. Without examining her own feelings, she went with him to Palestine. It was enough for her that they shared the same vision—Israel! Later she thought that Ezra had never had a dream, not even when they first joined the kibbutz. He had become the sheep expert while, for thirty years, she took care of the infants. In the beginning, they fought, or, to be precise, she fought and he remained silent. But with time, and in spite the lack of understanding, a careful, even tender love blossomed between them. And although lovemaking between them was awkward, hurried, and without satisfaction, she continued to make love with him again and again without passion, yet unable to stop. She was hit by feelings of guilt, sorrow, and resentment toward him as if they had missed some great opportunity. But she also knew that they were carrying between them a heavy weight that only the two of them together were able to carry.

A few days earlier, she asked Ezra to hand her a mirror. You don't need a mirror, you look fine, he had grumbled. But Marta insisted; so he brought the small hand mirror from the bathroom, laid it by her hand, and quickly left the room. She picked it up, hardly able to hold it. For a moment, she looked only at her hand. She shuddered. All her life, she was proud of her lovely hands, and now she saw dry skin, yellow and spotted: a dead hand. She wanted to cry, and decided not to look at her face. Never mind, she muttered, dropped the mirror, and shut her eyes.

Now, as always, she was thinking about her youngest daughter, Iris, who constantly hovered at the edge of her consciousness; Iris who had never been like other children; Iris whose face, since she was a baby, was clouded; Iris who never smiled, never played. She asked for nothing and accepted nothing; she seemed to be locked in a tight, place of lightness. Marta remembered how difficult it was to love Iris, what a tremendous effort it took even to communicate with the sullen, dark, little girl, who silently came out of her womb, and silently remained. Iris never once crawled onto her lap, or even cried. Sometimes during the day, Marta would go to the Toddlers' House and look at her daughter sitting alone in the corner, her eyes gazing blankly into the distance. In moments like that, Marta wanted to scream. Later in kindergarten, the children ignored her. At school, she sat alone. The children named her the Weird One.

The silent girl grew into a frozen young woman. Marta's heart burned with pain and guilt, the tears choking her throat as she watched Iris's empty face and wooden movements. Despite many wakeful nights, she, who knew all about children, didn't understand what was wrong with her daughter. Sometimes at night, she would try to talk to Ezra about it. But Ezra locked himself inside himself. I don't know any child psychology, he would say, and she angrily blamed him for not supporting her, for not caring enough. And then she would be ashamed of herself for the rage she unloaded on him, for she saw his eyes mist in pain and frustration as he watched their five-year-old gazing blankly into the distance, her eyes dark glass.

When Iris was eighteen years old, she slashed her wrists. That day, like any other day, Marta was working in the Children's House. She was bathing Guy, Dahlia's little boy, when Anna came running in. Marta! she gasped. It's Iris! Let's go! Hurry! Marta clasped little Guy to her chest and leaned against the wall, letting out a low sound. Anna took the baby from her arms. It's bad. Anna's voice came to Marta like an echo from her own belly. She saw Iris dead. Panic gripped her, and for a long moment, she was paralyzed with terror. Marta! Anna shook her shoulders. Marta, it's Iris! Marta, do you understand? Marta came out of her stupor. Ezra, she whispered. Does Ezra know? We sent Eli to fetch him from the field. Anna caught her hand. Let's go! she said.

When she saw Iris lying on the bed, red bandages on her wrists, her panic vanished. Her daughter needed her. Iris? She shook her daughter's shoulder lightly. Iris? Iris didn't respond. She's in shock. She heard Anna's voice from somewhere in the distance. Iris, it's me, Marta. Iris always called her Marta, never Mother. She bent down and kissed her daughter's forehead. It felt cold and dry. Marta held her daughter until the wailing of the ambulance penetrated their privacy. Her body tightened like that of a wounded animal.

On the way to the hospital, for the first time in her life, she pleaded with God. For forty-eight hours, Marta sat by her daughter's bed. Her two other children came to see their sister; but mostly they sat with their mother, holding her hand, trying to comfort her. She didn't hear or see them. Her eyes didn't leave Iris's face. All her senses were completely focused on the inert face, as if she was begging her daughter to allow her to share her loneliness. What did I do wrong? she asked herself repeatedly. But she knew the truth.

During her two-day watch at Iris's bedside, Marta grew to love her daughter in a new way, a soft, patient love —a love she had never felt before for her daughter. In sleep Iris's face lost its morbidity, her brow was smooth, her skin clear. And Marta noticed how long and thick Iris's eyelashes were. She thought of her daughter's eyes, huge almond-shaped brown eyes, now closed. Why did Iris reject life, she asked herself, tears running down her cheeks. Iris, my child, she whispered, speak to me.

Iris opened her eyes as if she heard her mother's words, and for one moment, Marta perceived a depth of pain that she had never seen there before. The corners of Iris's mouth turned down, and Marta couldn't tell if it was a smile or an expression of pain. Iris's hand moved, and Marta covered it with her own trembling hand. Mother, Iris said, I am going to have a baby. Then she closed her eyes. Iris, who had never called her mother, who had always been a mystery to her, became real. She sat there for hours, watching Iris's face, softly stroking her hand. Doctors and nurses came and went away. Her friends from the kibbutz brought her food and drinks, trying to persuade her to lie down and rest. And Marta made a tremendous effort to smile at everyone, but didn't answer. She didn't remove her eyes from Iris's face, and continued to stroke her hand. The thoughts were beating wildly in her head. Who did Iris sleep with? Who is responsible for her pregnancy? Was she raped? Will she ever have the courage to ask? And if she did ask, how would Iris respond? Frightened, she reined in her thoughts, tears burning in her throat.

In the evening, Ezra found her curled up on the bed, her face on the pillow next to Iris's head, both of them in a deep sleep. He stood there looking at them for a long time; lines of sorrow and love were etched deep in his face, his heart moaning in his chest. Suddenly, unexpectedly, Marta opened her eyes. She sat up. I fell asleep. She smiled at him confusedly, her cheeks turning red. Softly Ezra stroked her head, then bent, and kissed her lips. Shah . . . Sleep, he whispered, and hurried to leave the room. Through the open door, she saw him leaning against the hallway wall, his shoulders shaking—he was weeping like a child.

Seven months later, Iris gave birth to a healthy little girl. She named her Natanya, meaning a gift from God. For a moment a sad smile illuminated Marta's ravished face. She remembered the night she conceived Iris. It was raining. Phosphorescent snakes of lightning zigzagged across the sky. A wild wind shook the shutters. She tossed, unable to sleep. Ezra, in the other bed, was sleeping calmly, his breath coming in a soft whistle through his slightly opened lips. Suddenly she threw off her blanket. Ezra, she called. Ezra! Ezra's eyes fluttered. "Ha? Ha? What is it?" he muttered then resumed his sleep. She opened the door, welcoming the rain into their small room. The wind whistled in her ears, whipping her hair across her face into her eyes. Within seconds, she was drenched all over, her hair dripping. Something hard inside her melted; her skin shuddered with yearning and sensuality, as if the rain was the lover she always yearned for. She spread her arms and lifted her face, letting the rain caress her skin, lustily breathing in its wet-earth scent. Marta, for God's sake, close the door. You'll catch your death! She heard Ezra's voice. Ezra, she called; come, it's so exciting. But Ezra only grumbled and covered his head with the blanket.

She stood smiling, hearing her mother's voice saying the same words. Marta, for God's sake, you'll catch your death, child. Close the door. Her mother's voice was loving and concerned; and when Marta came back into the house, her mother, who too had loved to stand in the rain, was waiting for her with a glass of hot milk and a towel. But most vividly, she remembered her mother's embracing smile and the little house where she grew up, and her father, and someone caressing her head, the feeling of belonging and calmness.

After a while, she came back into the room, took off her soaking nightgown, and rubbed her hair with a towel. She looked at Ezra. She was surprised to see his eyes open, his hands clasped behind his head—he was watching her.

What is it? What are you staring at? she asked, feeling suddenly shy. You are beautiful, he said. She giggled, feeling like a young girl. He had never said she looked beautiful. Not when he proposed to her, not when they got married, not when their children were born. His unexpected words made her tremble with anticipation. It has been years since her body wakened with desire. Now she wanted to be swept away by her mounting excitement. She dropped the towel then, trembling, got into his bed, hoping this time it will be like in her dreams, like love should be. But as usual, he hurried to take her. And while he was moaning and sweating above her, she listened to the rain splattering against the windows and fancied that her soul left her body there on the bed and soared. She imagined herself being carried away on a cloud, singing the songs of her youth.

Afterward, she stayed awake and listened to the wind. Her excitement at Ezra's words, You're beautiful, melted away and was replaced by a deep loneliness. That night, Iris was conceived. Marta was forty-two when she conceived Iris, Ezra forty-eight, and looking so young. Where his face was smooth and tanned, hers was dry and lined like a spider's web. His belly was strong and hard; hers sagged from childbearing. His hair was thick and shiny, her own thinning and stricken with gray. But she consoled herself that his soul was dull and his heart was timid, while hers was vivacious and daring. Tears ran down her cheeks. The pain in her chest was squeezing her heart in a death grip. She was thinking of the relief death would bring her if only she could let go. She had never feared life; she didn't fear death. Why then was she so stubbornly clinging to a life that had become insulting? She knew the answer, for her granddaughter, for Nati. Her pain lessened, and her breathing eased. Whenever she thought of Nati, the pain became more tolerable as though the six-year-old girl fought for her grandmother's life. Sometimes she entertained the thought that Nati was an angel looking after her. God, she whispered, if you are there anywhere and if you care, watch over my Nati. Again she remembered Iris's lifeless face, and the bloody bandages floated in front of her eyes. Her breathing became raspy, and she had a coughing fit. On the white sheet that covered her, she saw her own blood.

For three months after Nati's birth, Iris became like a watchdog. She seemed transfigured by motherhood, focused on something outside herself for the first time. She didn't let the infant out of her sight. She clung to the baby tenaciously. Marta tried to reassure her that no one would take Nati away from her, but Iris lived in constant terror. She kept Nati locked with her in the house. At night, the infant slept in her arms. She put ribbons in the baby's hair, made little frocks for her, prepared her food herself because she didn't have milk to nurse. The only person she trusted with Nati was Marta. But when Marta held the baby in her arms, she felt her daughter's eyes sink into her flesh. Then things changed again:

One Friday evening, when all the members of the kibbutz had gathered in the dining hall to light the Sabbath candles and sing Sabbath songs, she went to Iris's house to see Nati. The house was dark. She opened the door. Iris! she called. There was no answer. When she turned on the light, she saw Nati lying on the bed in soiled diapers, whimpering miserably, flailing her tiny fists in the air. Iris was sitting on the bed, staring blankly into the distance. Iris? Marta said softly. Slowly Iris turned to her. Her eyes were dark glass. Marta, she said, her voice flat, her face a mask, I can't.

I know, Marta said, longing to take her daughter in her arms, to tell her she loved her and that all would be fine. Her arms reached out to Iris, then dropped back to her sides. She remembered that Iris couldn't bear being touched. Marta focused her attention on Nati instead, and while she cleaned the baby and changed her diapers, she hummed a song that she used to sing to Iris when she was a baby. Then, with Nati in her arms, she turned and said quietly, I'm taking Nati home with me. Iris didn't react.

When Ezra came home that night and saw the little girl, he didn't ask any questions. He sat down on the bed and softly caressed Nati's cheek with the back of his index finger. When she's grown, he said, I'll take her to the fields with the sheep. It's better than being with people. Don't talk nonsense, said Marta. But in her heart of hearts, she wondered if he wasn't right. The next day, she brought Nati to the Children's House. Her one consolation was that Nati would be safe.

After that Friday, Iris rarely left her house. Marta brought Nati to her every evening. Sometimes Iris played with the baby; sometimes she only gazed at her. But as Nati grew, Iris and she became more connected. Iris would tell Nati stories from the Bible. or sing to her, in a gentle voice, songs that little girls sing, and on those occasions, affection of a different sort flowed between them. And Nati would sit across from her mother, wishing their time together would last forever. But more often than not, during Nati's visits, Iris would stand silently by the window, staring with glazed eyes at the pecan tree that never gave fruit. Nati would play under the pecan tree close to the house. And while she listened to a noisy chorus of crickets, she would watch the window and hope that her mother would call her, smile at her, be like other mothers were. After a while, she would go back to Marta's house, her head bowed and her light curls covering most of her little face. Ezra was always there waiting for her. He would swipe her up in his arms and hoist her to his shoulders, and she would urge him, like she was spurring a horse. Dio! she would shout, laughing and crying, embracing his neck tightly with her tiny arms, and he would melt.

Nati was five when Marta became ill. Once she knew that nothing could be done for her at the hospital, she told her doctor that she wanted to die at home. A few days later, she was back in her own bed. Iris, who couldn't bear the hospital, would now come every day. She would arrive at three and leave at five. She was never late and never early. She would sit on the straight-backed chair by the closed window, her hands clasped between her knees, her eyes fastened to her mother's in silence.

At first, Marta would talk. She told Iris about her childhood in Poland, about her own mother and how much she had loved her. She told her daughter about her meeting with Ezra at the Zionist camp and how he proposed to her. Oh, Iris, she smiled, he was so handsome. And she talked for hours about her early days in Kibbutz Regev. Those were wondrous days, she said musingly. We had nothing; we lived in tents; we almost drowned in the swamps. Many died of malaria and typhoid fever. But we had a dream. It seemed to us that the God of Moses was right there with us. The God of freedom. We were in our glory. Nothing scared us, not the scorching sun, not the scarcity of food and water, not even the malaria and typhoid fever, not death itself. We worked and sang and dreamed. Oh yes, she sighed, we had a dream.

Iris would sit there in silence, her eyes fastened on Marta's lips, an unexpected serenity softened her face. From time to time, the corners of her lips would quiver, and Marta recalled her daughter's face that time in the hospital, that one time when she had called her mother. Was this a smile or a grimace of pain? She still didn't know. And yet Iris's silent presence gave Marta a sense of comfort until one day she forgot herself, and the question erupted from her mouth. Iris, my child, who is Nati's father?

Iris glared at her, her eyes wild and panic-stricken. Extreme effort was etched on her face, and Marta saw the conflict that erupted in her daughter's mind. Iris's mouth opened and closed, but not a sound came out. Marta waited, her eyes fixed on her daughter's wild eyes. Iris, she whispered. Iris stood up. For a long moment, she dug deep into the green eyes fixed upon her; and Marta saw how her daughter's face shut, her body froze, and she was standing there lost—her eyes dark glass. Her heart sinking, Marta saw her daughter vanishing, dissolving in front of her eyes.

For a long time, she lay there looking at the empty chair. For four days now, Iris hadn't come to visit her. For four days, the chair remained empty. Marta! Marta! She heard suddenly a voice calling her name, forcing her to surface, not to give up. She opened her eyes. Anna, her friend, was placing a food tray on a small table beside her bed. How do you feel, Marta? asked Anna, placing a cool hand on the hot, sweat- drenched forehead. Have you seen Nati? Marta asked. Yes, she and Little Micha are collecting snails and rain worms by the dining hall. Anna's eyes were fixed on the red spot on Marta's sheet. She stuffed her hands quickly into her apron pockets and tried not to stare at the bloodstains.

What's to eat? Marta tried to say with a light voice. Anna's face lit up. With a trembling hand, she pushed away a strand of gray hair from her forehead. As usual, she said, chicken soup, chicken, and potatoes. What else is new? smiled Marta. But after two spoons of soup, she sighed, fatigued. As much as she wished to please Anna, she couldn't eat. She looked at Anna apologetically. Anna took the food away. Never mind, she said. Don't force yourself. After a moment, she asked, Is Ezra home? Baaaa, bleated Marta weakly. At that moment, the door burst open. Nati came running in, her face smeared with mud, her eyes excited, full of light. In her hand was an assortment of wildflowers from the field. For you, Grandma, she laughed and scattered the flowers on Marta's bed, then immediately flung open the shutters. Grandma, she chirped, I saw three rainbows today, three rainbows, Grandma! And I collected so many rain worms and snails. Dahlia was really mad because we got muddy, and Daphna crushed the worms in her hand, and then she wanted to catch a rainbow and cried when she couldn't. Silly girl! Doesn't she know that you can't catch a rainbow? Nati gulped a mouthful of air. Do you know the story of Noah and the ark, Grandma? She hiccupped. Mother once told it to me. Oh, Grandma, it was such a wonderful story. All those big animals, lions and elephants and giraffes. But Mother said that Noah took mosquitoes and ants too. I wish she would tell me more stories. Well—she gulped another breath— I can ask Grandpa. He knows everything. He told me so. He said he was a teacher, like Dahlia, when he lived in Poland. Grandma, where's Poland? A long way away, said Marta. Very far? Yes, Nati, very, very far. Oh. Nati lifted her eyebrows and crinkled her nose. Are rainbows because God promised Noah in the Bible never to make a flood anymore? Mother said so. Yes, Nati. Marta found a voice inside herself that was free of illness, a confident voice for her granddaughter only. Well, said Nati, if God promised not to make floods anymore, how come Rita's house was flooded yesterday? How come, Grandma? God should keep his promises, shouldn't he, Grandma? She puckered her lips and waited. But Marta couldn't answer. She felt her lungs and heart being crushed.

Grandma! Nati tugged at her hand. Why didn't God keep his promise? Why did Rita's house flood? The child picked a flower from the blanket and put it next to Marta's cheek. She placed a marigold in Marta's hand, and Marta inhaled the fragrance of open fields and wet earth. Her fingers fondled the delicate petals of the marigold. Her breathing eased.

Little Micha said it was a lot of fun to have the house flooded, said Nati. He bragged that he could swim in the living room. I know he wanted me to admire him; it must have been fun. Do you think God might flood our house too? She shrugged her tiny shoulders. I hope he does. I hope he doesn't keep his promise. People don't. And anyway, maybe God is sick. She thought for a moment. God is sick, she declared, otherwise, he'd make you well. Mother says God can do everything.

Maybe he forgot, Marta said. A pout puckered Nati's face. She said, Grandpa promised to take me to the fields today, but he forgot—just like God. No, Nati. He didn't forget, said Anna. He didn't want you to get wet and catch a cold. Grandpa loves you very much. Nati frowned. She looked at Anna, then again at Marta. After a moment, she asked Marta, Didn't you tell Anna that on Saturday you got up from bed and we stood in the rain and I held you by myself and we got wet? No, it's our secret, smiled Marta. Oh! Nati's eyes opened wide. Our own secret, she said in a conspiratorial voice. But I thought it's only a secret from Mother. Don't worry, Nati, said Marta. Anna will keep our secret. Marta closed her eyes. The light in the room was white and harsh, and hurt her eyelids like thousands of multi-colored needles. Nati, she said, please close the door and the shutters.

It isn't good for you to be in the dark all day Nati declared suddenly. She climbed on the narrow bed, cuddled close to Marta, and stuck her thumb in her mouth. Her shiny brown curls mingled on the pillow with Marta's gray hair. Marta turned on her side, and, for a moment, held the little body to her chest. A sudden, mysterious warmth flooded her cold body. She closed her eyes and, for a moment, smiled deliciously.

Grandma. Yes, my child? Make me an omelet. Nati didn't remove the thumb from her mouth. Anna stood up as though in obedience to a command. Are you hungry, Nati? Marta asked. Yes, Nati said, and you make the best omelet in the world. You know, the one with the jam. Today, Anna will make your omelet. Marta's voice was soft and calm, but Anna saw the defeat in her green eyes. Marta's body under the bed cover was hardly visible: a suggestion of a person. Her face was white, but her cheeks glowed red with fever. From time to time, a cough wracked her body. There were several spots of blood on the sheet now. No, no, Grandma, Nati insisted. You can make it. I know you can. Get up, Grandma. Grandma, get up already. Please!

Anna, Marta called. Anna was at her side instantly. Help me up, Marta said. Without a word, Anna helped her out of bed. As she supported her friend, Anna suddenly thought of the clay vase she had inherited from her own mother. The other day, she took it off the shelf intending to dust it, and it crumbled between her fingers. Now, with great care, Anna held Marta. Nati hovered around them like a bright butterfly anxiously giving orders. No, no, Grandma, not that one. The one that Little Micha's mother made, that one over there, the red one. Anna reached for the strawberry jam; she placed it on the counter in front of Marta. She broke the eggs with one hand while supporting her almost-lifeless friend with the other.

No, Nati said. Grandma has to make the omelet. Do it, Grandma! Her voice was angry, but Marta heard the terror inside the child's body. And the love. Her fingers felt clumsy and stiff, as slowly, silently, she beat the eggs. A heavy fatigue spread through her blood, paralyzing her limbs. For a moment, all her wishes died; and she longed to be in bed, to sleep for a long time inside the silence, to be one with the void—since, behind it, there is no guilt, there is no pain. Her eyelids dropped; her head sank onto her chest. She made a tremendous effort to clear the fog that settled in her brain and accept what was happening to her. She lifted up her head and forced her eyes open, and as she poured the yellow mixture into the pan, she became acutely aware of daffodil and narcissus fragrance drifting in the air. Ezra, she called silently, I want Ezra. Then her legs began to shake, and she felt Anna's arms holding her up, almost lifting her off the floor.

Grandma. Nati pulled at her arm. You're burning the omelet. When she turned the omelet with a spatula, she gazed out of the open kitchen window, her eyes filled with wintry brilliance. Odd, she thought, the light seemed less vivid than she knew it to be after rain, as though a fog had moved in. The colors of the trees faded, as well as the mountain hues, as though a mist had moved in and subdued the light. I know the light is bright and blue, she was thinking, forcing herself to see again the radiance. In vain. The light remained muted.

Almost done. Now the jam. She heard Anna's voice as an echo in her ear. Slowly, silently, Marta spread the jam, while her mind was fastened on the time when she worked in the Children's House, rubbing baby oil on pure limbs. Nati squeezed her body between the two women, clasping Marta's waist with her arms and pressing her cheek into her grandmother's back as if she wished to inhabit her grandma and give her warmth and life from her own young body.

I'll hold Grandma, she said, her little arms tightening around Marta. Suddenly, as though a mysterious hand was at work, the mist lifted, the window brimmed with brilliant light. A sensation of lightness, as if she were nothing but air, came upon her. A scent of fields was thick in her nostrils. She looked at the distant mountains—standing, as though hanging between earth and sky, silent and pure, almost white, glimmering in the white light. In her mind's eye, she saw the silvery glint of the leaves on the olive trees in summer. Somewhere a dog barked.

More jam, said Nati. The child's voice entered Marta's body and stayed there. More, more, said Nati. It'll burst, Marta said, her eyes wide-open, taking leave of the clouds and the trees and the birds and the mountains. She heard Nati's voice saying into her back, Let it burst. Okay. Marta coughed then whispered, Nati, you're holding me too tight. Reluctantly, Nati let go of Marta's waist; and slowly, so slowly, Marta turned around. Here, my child, she said, her voice lifting with pride, is the king of an omelet. And as she handed Nati the plate with the fat yellow omelet oozing red jam, her hands were as steady as the mountains.

I knew you could make it, Grandma, Nati said. Who said I couldn't? said Marta. The room whirled around her. She was falling. Anna caught her, and cradling her like a baby in her strong arms, she carried her back to bed. From her bed, Marta watched as Nati ate the omelet slowly, licking the last bit of strawberry jam off her fingers without once taking her eyes from Marta's face. Those big almond-shaped brown eyes: Iris's eyes. When she finished eating, she climbed onto Marta's bed, kissed Marta's cracked lips, jumped off, called good-bye to Anna, and ran to the opened door. She halted at the door, turned back to the room, and announced, I am going to Little Micha's house now. Rita is baking cookies, and she said I can help her. She turned her attention outside. Oh, look, Grandma, it's raining again. Marta's lips moved to reply, but Nati was already outside, running toward Little Micha's house.

Anna went to shut the door. Leave it open, Marta said. Anna remained standing at the foot of the bed for a long while. Marta tried to smile. She spoke no more. Suddenly she felt a familiar presence, two hands holding hers with strange softness that seeped into her body, enfolding her in a dreamy quiet. Ezra? But it was not Ezra. Her eyelids lifted, and her eyes sunk into two huge almond-shaped brown eyes. She saw a wet face, a mouth trembling. Was it a grimace or a smile? She still couldn't tell. Iris, my child. Her lips moved, but not a word came out. Her eyelids dropped. Mother. She hesitated. Then as if through a mist, her hand lifted, and she caressed her daughter's face.

Her hand fell. She floated. The sun's rays shone through the open door and made Marta's pain turn vague, almost friendly, the room very bright. She saw her mother standing just outside the door in the rain, a smile on her face, her arms outstretched. Someone was playing the harmonica, and the bittersweet music of her youth filled the room. Someone is waiting for me, Marta thought. Where is Ezra? But she knew. Ezra was where he belonged, in the green pastures tending the sheep, dreaming of plump women with ripe breasts. Martha smiled, her eyes open. Outside the rain grew louder.

It is hard to write. Sometimes you completely disappear and it confuses me. The past becomes distant and alien. The longing has become a dull, non-existent echo –a hollow, just there in the belly. Not an oppressive or screaming hollow, sometimes it only whistles a distant, barely recognizable tune. Am I exaggerating? Maybe. So where are you, and where am I? That too will eventually become clear. But perhaps not, and perhaps it is just a dream: and when I wake I will see all my friends again, we will join hands, all ten of us, dance and sing our old songs. Perhaps we will be lying on the lawn and stare at the huge familiar stars and wonder; what it is all about, this world we live in?

CHAPTER 16

Micha

BUT HERE I SHOULD LEAVE MYSELF FOR A moment and get into something else. I would like to tell you about a little boy (I knew his parents well. Especially his mother, Rita.) and how he tells the story of his childhood to his Mother.

Micha woke up, his heart booming, his body covered by sticky sweat, tears in his eyes. The nightmare had visited him again and again. He felt like couldn't go on like this, or he would be finished. He must go there, to the 'Rocky Hill,' and tell her the entire story of that time during the war, when it all happened. In the dark of the army hut he dressed hurriedly, and in few minutes he was out and running through the starlit night. The army camp was not far from the kibbutz. On the way he stopped to gather wild flower that grew in abandon beside the empty road. When he finally arrived at the 'Rocky Hill,' he flopped exhausted on her stone side. He waited few minutes in order to regain his breath, then began to talk:

I brought you the flowers you loved so much, and I can hear you saying, flowers should stay where they belong, in the ground. And you have filled every empty spot in the house with potted plants and growing flowers, and said; if I truly, truly wanted to, I could speak to the roots and watch the flowers grow. And when Father said; don't put crazy ideas into the child's head, you ignored him. But you see, I remembered about the flowers, and I dug them out with the roots -so I can plant them here where the ground is fresh and damp, like after the rain, which you loved so much.

Remember when life seemed forever like a dream? And it was all right to leave the children at home alone, and people didn't lock the doors because the kibbutz was a safe place, or so everyone thought, and every day we played in the fields, and the mornings were always blue and the birds screamed in the branches of the trees, and fragrance of wildflowers wafted in the air, and millions of snails and earthworms appeared after the rain, and a honey sun smiled at us, painting our hair with gold, and eyes and face, sprinkling our noses with big brown spots.

And then the wars started, and the boys wanted to be paratroopers, and in class we read the Bible every day because we were told it was our heritage and history. And

Old Gera was still alive, and Sam the Cat was slinking around, and Father's hair was still brown and his tanned face taut. And Nati was a mischievous tiny girl, whom, at age seven, I was crazy about.

But it was not in order to tell you this, I have run away from the army camp and came here all messed up and sweating and without breath. I came to tell you finally about that night when a storm rampaged outside, and I was so scared, and you weren't there. I still have nightmares about that night, and that crazy memorial day keeps haunting me like a demon from Dante's Inferno, and I want to tell you how it was then when I was only a little boy. Maybe, only maybe, it will ease the pain. Wherever you are, Mother, listen well. This time listen really well.

Once when I was about seven, I was lying on my stomach on the floor of my room, trying to concentrate on a jigsaw puzzle, waiting for Nati to come and play with me; but outside the wind roared like a beast, and the windows shook, and I heard sounds like moans around the house, and I knew that Nati would never make it in that storm. But in spite of my anxiety, I smiled because one never knew what Nati was up to; she was mischievous and daring and loved adventures—never afraid of anything. Maybe she contained a little of her mother, because sometimes, in the midst of a game, she would suddenly say, I have to go now, my mother is waiting, and I would notice how her face became suddenly white and tense, and sometimes her lips trembled. You adored Nati; you would hug her and kiss her and say, Natushka, you are so pretty. And then you would sigh and say; I always wanted a girl, and I was a little jealous.

But you never loved anyone like you love Big Micha, even after he left you and joined the dead. I could never understand why you wasted so much love on a dead man. And after you weren't with us anymore, father hardly ever spoke, and his hair turned white, and his face cracked, and his eyes—it's difficult for me to describe his eyes because suddenly there was nothing in his eyes. So if eyes can be empty, Father's eyes were empty after what you have done. Most of the time, he wandered like a spirit in the olive grove, or sat near the window with the view of the lawn, the acacia tree, the daisies, and the daffodils; and when I spoke to him, he would look at me and say, confused, What, what did you say, child? At such moments, I could have killed you myself.

Sometimes Nati would come and, for a few moments, relieve father from the depression that set upon him like a beast. She told stories about the fields, the sheep, and the jokes of her grandfather, Ezra, whom she loved even more than she had loved her grandmother, Marta, who died of cancer. After her grandmother died, Nati said that it is all right because her grandmother is now in a place full of light, and rain falls there all the time. Her grandmother was crazy about rain; she said the rain is the essence of life.

The thought that Nati wouldn't come because of the storm made me stand up abruptly and upset the puzzle, and I looked at the mess of little cardboard pieces and snorted in disgust and screwed up my eyes and bared my teeth and screamed, I'm a tiger! I'm a man-eating beast! I roared, running around the room with claws ready to gouge out the enemy's eyes. Then I was Sam the Cat, and I crouched on the floor and arched my back, feeling the hair bristle on my neck, and didn't make a sound. My whole body tensed, ready for war. But the moment I sprang into the air, ready to catch my prey, I began to wheeze and choke and collapsed on the floor. Again I was only a little boy with asthma—a questionable amusement, especially when you are all alone in a house you suddenly distrust.

I turned on the radio, hoping music would distract me—even the news, anything. But the radio roared and whistled as if a whole pack of hounds and hyenas were caught inside it, so I turned it off and ran to the window. I watched how the wind teased the clouds, and the whole world was charged with electricity as furious bolts of lightning struck a messy sky, followed by stupendous booms and distant rumbles. And I couldn't shut the loosely hinged shutters that were banging against the wall of the house. As the wind intensified, I was certain the house swayed. And when I looked at the clock, it was only a little past six, and you were still out because it was your turn to work in the dining hall. And I imagined you standing behind the stainless steel counter handing out steaming dishes, and I could smell the peas and the roast potatoes and the chicken, and I saw your face shining with sweat and your hands slippery with grease and your green eyes dull and gray and full of fatigue.

I knew how much you loathed working in the dining hall, because the first thing you did when you came home was to kick off your shoes and rub your toes, and complain that your legs were swollen and your feet were sore, and that you smelled of garlic and rancid oil. Disgusting, I remember you saying once, your face contorted with distaste. And father looked at you and said with this special smile he kept only for you, You're so spoiled, Rita. You stared at him, and I saw your eyes narrow. Wise guy, you said, your voice scratchy , and Father said, I didn't mean to upset you. And when he brought you a cup of coffee, you pushed away his hand. Be careful, he said, and the smile was gone from his face. You said you were sorry, and I stuck my fingers deep into my ears from dread that you'd fight again. Michal'e, you said, take your fingers out of your ears.

It isn't healthy. And you asked; did you water the plants? and I muttered aha, and you smiled at me, and I saw a net of tiny wrinkles around your eyes.

But worst of all were the nights when you were too exhausted to sit on my bed and sing to me because, when you sang to me, your small soft voice made me feel so . . . But here I always reach the boundary of my thoughts because, at the age of seven, I didn't have words to articulate my feelings when you sang to me.

And Father was at a secretariat meeting where he spent most of his time arguing with Old Gera about winter crops and the critical (I didn't know then what critical meant) water problem, and whether they should keep or get rid of the olive grove, or how many new members the kibbutz could absorb this year.

And that horrible night, when I felt as if there was no one, nothing in the entire world except the storm, and the thought of you and Father, set off a memory—a memory as distinct as the sound of the thunder that shook the windows, a memory of an early summer evening when I was playing with my tanks and soldiers in a corner of the living room. At that particular evening, you and Father had returned from the dining hall a little later than usual, and Father settled at his usual place, a small table under the window, with the view of the lawn and the acacia tree and the daisies and the daffodils and opened the newspaper. You placed a plate full of freshly baked cookies on the table, which filled the room with aroma of vanilla, pecans and raisins. Enjoy, Eli, you said. And then you came over to me and cupped my chin and lifted my face to yours and kissed me on my lips and gave me two cookies, and I swallowed them hardly chewing. Take it easy, Michal'e, you said, there are plenty, and you laughed and gave me another kiss. Then you went and stood by the little gas stove, waiting for the water to boil for coffee.

You looked so pretty, dressed in a white silk shirt and new blue jeans. Your hair loose, fell in waves and tangles all the way to your shoulders, and your eyes sparkled green and deep. I couldn't take my eyes off you. I prayed in my heart that you'd look at me, but you poured a cup of coffee for Father and asked; how was your day, Eli? Without lifting his eyes from the paper, father said, Like any other day, arguments, endless arguments. You laughed and said, Is that so? It seems to me that all you ever do in those meetings is argue. Father didn't think it was funny. He said; yeah, so it seems, and he began tapping with his teaspoon on the cookie plate, a habit that drove you nuts until you said, and your voice was cutting, stop it, Eli. And he stopped. After that you and Father sat for a time and didn't speak at all, only drank the bitter coffee, and you didn't laugh any more.

I continued to play with my tanks and soldiers, imagining myself a general in the commando unit, my soldiers charging heroically, and my tanks perfectly lined up ready to attack, and corpses are strewn all over the battlefield, and the enemy almost defeated. Fire! Fire! I shouted and clapped my hands together, a habit keeping the palms of my hands always slightly red. Remember? And you said suddenly, and your voice was sharp as hail, Michal'e, why do you always play war? Go play outside, it's healthier. And I was stunned by your sudden anger. I had been playing war for as long as I could remember myself. All the boys played war. And all I could think to say was *because*, and you looked at me suspiciously and said, because why? Don't be a wise guy with me. And your outburst confused me, so, I had to restrain myself from crying. And then father lifted his eyes from the paper and said, because boys play war, Rita. You didn't say anything and began to eat the cookies very fast and didn't pay attention to the crumbs falling on the table and on the floor around your chair, and I was so surprised because I have never seen you eating in such a wild way. You were always so pedantic and neat—even compulsively so in my opinion.

Suddenly father's voice thundered; listen! Rita! You stopped eating the cookies and looked at him with startled eyes, and my eyelids began to twitch. And you said, Don't yell, Eli, I'm not deaf. And my father said that important decisions should be made by the younger generation. Again you told him not to yell and asked him what was he talking about, and he said that he was talking about the last secretariat meeting and how the old people had been driving him insane with their archaic ideas. I saw how the line between your eyebrows deepened, and you asked why. And father said; leave it up to them and we'd be back to using mules and ploughs. I tell you, Rita, older people should know when it's time to quit and make room for younger people. You should hear the nostalgia in their voices when they talk about the good old days, when they still lived in tents and didn't have electricity or running water. You would think they had a feast then instead of swamps, malaria, and typhoid fever.

And you were silent for a long time, gazing into space with lamenting eyes; then suddenly you said, in a voice that made me wish I could run to you and hug you, that their good old days sound so romantic, and that now our men die in wars and our children play war. War, always war. Is it better to die in a war, Eli? And the pitch of your voice was unusually high and tense, and your eyes saturated with sadness. I know, I know, Father said, wars are terrible, but it's time for the kibbutz to change. The pioneering days are long over. Without looking at him, you said, You have a stone for a heart, Eli, and you began talking about the days when you and Big Micha had spent many summer dawns in the olive grove, watching the sunlight play on the Judean hills. Each time, you said, the hills looked different. Sometimes clear and close, other times covered with clouds or fog, but—and your voice became hushed and silky,—"the real magic came at night when... You didn't finish your sentence because father roared; enough! This thing has got to stop! And he stood up abruptly, shoving the chair in enormous anger. And you continued to talk about your nights in the olive grove with Big Micha as if you were alone in the world. Then Father's elbow hit the cup, spilling the coffee, which spread in a big blotch on the tablecloth. Damn it, Rita, shut up! he shouted and, with shaking fingers, lit a cigarette. I heard him breathing hard. I thought in my heart that you weren't fair, were even cruel, and I didn't want to think of you that way.

And Father began wandering about the room; stopped in front of your chair and said, Big Micha, that's all you're able to think about. You haven't heard a word I've said. This thing has got to stop for the child's sake and mine. And you sat stiff and still, your eyes following the coffee stain spreading on the tablecloth, until at last you looked at him and said; you shouldn't have married me, Eli. And I saw how Father's smooth face suddenly turned ashen and terribly sad, and he said in a strange voice; Rita, I love you. You lifted to him a drained face and said that you were terribly sorry for your outburst and that this had been a terrible day, and you're so tired. And then you picked up the newspaper and glanced at the headlines and said, Bad news, it's so terrible, all this bombing and killing and hate and— But again you didn't finish your words because father snatched the paper out of your hands, and lifted you from the chair, and pulled you to him, and pressed your body tightly to his. Rita, Rita, he said, and his heavy face was buried in your hair. I didn't like it. You were so tiny and seemed so breakable, and he was so big and rough. It seemed to me that one of his hands could cover your whole body, and I was terrified that he might break you. And you said, I'm sorry, Eli, so sorry, and by the shaking of your shoulders, I knew that you were weeping, weeping with your face pressed against his massive chest. And he caressed your hair and kept saying, It's all right, it's all right, but his voice sounded like when you walk on gravel.

And while you and Father were carrying on, I sat in the corner of the room and trembled, and I felt the blood drumming in my temples and was dizzy and confused because I didn't understand anything from what I heard. I was sure that you had completely forgotten my presence in the room, and as always, when you behaved this way, my throat choked and my chest tightened. I longed to see you laughing and happy and light and shimmering like the skin of your face and arms and belly and legs, but you were sad, always sad or angry.

And when I no longer could bear the tension, I left my soldiers and tanks scattered on the floor and went outside and sat on the lawn and threw stones at Sam the Cat. And there was the cat, and there I was. And for a while, we stood growling and hissing and baring our teeth, and then I heard you calling through the open window, Michal'e; again you're abusing the cat? Let him be, it's time for bed. If you hurry, I'll read you a story. But I didn't move. I don't want a story, I said, I want you to sing to me, and I heard you sigh. Not tonight, you said in a nervous voice. I'm tired. And when I still didn't move, you said in this irritating voice, *My sweetheart*. But I insisted that you sing to me, and said, lie by me for only few minutes, Mama. And you pleaded; Come in, Michal'e, now, please, and your eyes were green again.

That night, I won. You sat on my bed and read to me a sad story about a boy named David Copperfield and sang about raisins and almonds, about the moon and the fields, and then you lay down at my side and fell asleep while I stayed awake and watched over you. At that moment, we were only the two of us, alone, bonded together. And I didn't know when I fell asleep and you returned to your room.

The next day, when I got home from school, I couldn't find my soldiers and tanks. They were not in their usual place in the wooden box under the bed, and I searched the entire house, but they disappeared. I didn't ask anything, only went to the bathroom, locked the door with the key, sat on the toilet, and cried.

And on that stormy night, when those thoughts sucked me in and you were not there, I imagined myself as a bird flying far, far away. And you? You thinking of me and missing me and crying and pleading and calling me to come back to you. And suddenly a terrible thought struck me—what if you'll forget me? Never again think of me? And I couldn't hold back, and wet my pants like a baby. I ran to my room, and banged the door shut, and peeled off my pants, and washed my legs that stunk of urine, and changed into my pajamas, and kicked the evidence of my shame under the bed. And shivering, I hid under the blanket and covered my head with the pillow, desperately trying not to think, shutting off the boom of the thunder that became a distant rumble that turned into the loud, clear voice of my father saying to you what I often heard him say; an accident, it's always an accident. What are we going to do about these accidents? And you answered, it will pass, it will pass. Give the child time. And father said; it is so embarrassing. He's already seven years old and in second grade. He should be sleeping in the Children's House like the other children, but no, he has to sleep at home because he still wets his bed. What are we going to do with him? And you said; these things happen you know, and besides, I like it that he sleeps at home. If they'd ask my opinion, all the children would sleep at home. And Father said, we've been discussing this matter in the secretariat meetings. Many parents want the children home at night. We've decided to bring this particular problem to a general vote next Saturday. Personally, I'm against it. And you said, but, Eli, you're always talking about changes, big changes. And my father answered, well, some things should not change, and this is one of them. The children's place is in the Children's House, together. It heightens their sense of communal spirit and toughens them up. But all this aside for the moment, what do you intend to do about the child? What is the matter with him? And you said, I don't know, Eli, I just don't know. You thought for a moment then said, We probably should take him to see a psychologist, and it sounded to me like some kind of a conspiracy. And there under my blanket, in the dark, I imagined you shaking your head and sighing, and I saw your face clearly, and my panic intensified, and I began to think that you'd never come home. So I tossed back the blanket and sat up shaking and snatched the pillow and clutched it to my chest and thought that I didn't want to go to a psychologist, that I didn't even know what a psychologist meant. And I shouted, no, determined not to cry no matter what.

For a moment, I forgot the fear and anxiety. For a moment, I forgot the lightning and thunder and decided to play with my football. Yes, I shouted, and clapped my hands and jumped off the bed, and ran to take out the ball from the closet. But then I froze, alarmed, as if someone invisible caught me from behind. And I stood there staring at the closet door, and remembered that only a few days ago I broke two of your geranium pots when I played ball in the room, and you were so angry I thought you'd never forgive me. I wet my bed every night, and father grumbled and grumbled. And with these thoughts, the sudden surge of energy left my body, and I banged my fists on the closet door, and kicked it with my foot, and hurt my big toe and shouted, shit! And I didn't even care that I promised you never to say that word. I found no relief. Only the rain was beating on the roof, and it sounded like horses' hooves stamping above my head. And I was sure the world was going to end any moment now, but you weren't there to protect me.

Angry with the rain, and angry with my father, and angry with you, and furious with the entire dark universe, I took out a big sheet of paper and my crayons, and crouched on the floor on my knees, and drew a figure of a man who resembled the man in the picture on your little bedside table. And above the picture I scribbled a name in black letters. And then I went to your desk and opened the drawer and took out a pair of sharp scissors that you warned me never to touch, and gouged the picture's eyes, and cut off his nose and mouth and ears. Then violently, I beheaded him. I plucked each finger separately, and severed the right arm, then the left. Then I removed the legs and the feet, and I cut the body into four equal parts. And when I had finished gouging, cutting, tearing and severing, I scooped up the pieces and tossed them into the air and blew on them with all my might and clapped my hands and shouted, go away, go away! And I looked up and saw the parts of the mutilated body hovering for a moment above me, and I covered my head with my hands, and then I saw him flutter to the floor and lie there. And his gouged eyes stared at me, and the hole of the mouth smirked at me in an impudent and leering way, and my whole body shuddered. So I picked up the pieces, one by one, and ran to the bathroom and threw them down the toilet, and flushed the water, and said, there! And my heart was threatening to burst from my body. Then I went back to the living room and took the fuzzy red blanket from the sofa and wrapped it around myself and sat down and pressed my knees to my chest and tried to imagine myself as a fuzzy, big, red bug. But it wasn't any good to pretend, because I remained a little boy. And then a blinding white flash flooded the room, and I squeezed my eyes shut, and clapped my hands to my ears. and felt the impact shaking my body. I said out loud, it's only thunder, and I tried to whistle, but I couldn't move my lips. I looked at the clock again and saw that it was only seven, and you weren't going to be back for two hours yet.

And so I wrapped myself tighter in the red blanket and dropped my head on the back of the sofa and closed my eyes and tried to breathe slowly, in and out, in and out, through the nose, softly, like Dr. Shoham taught me to do when I didn't feel good. But it didn't help, and my mind was swimming with images of strange and dark and horrifying scenes. I saw a huge, shapeless body coming right at me from the silence of the Rocky Hill, where Big Micha's body is buried, and I shook my head to shatter the image, and sucked air into my lungs, opened my eyes wide and vowed to myself never to close them again until you were home. And the confusion in my head became enormous, because as long as I remember myself, I heard people say that Big Micha wasn't buried on Rocky Hill at all because his body was blown to pieces while he parachuted over Jerusalem toward the Ammunition Hill during the Six-Day War, and he couldn't be identified. In those days, I couldn't understand why the name Micha Oren was engraved in the big stone on Rocky Hill, and they said it was symbolic, but what does a seven-year-old boy know about things being symbolic?

Oh, Mother, I was so scared, just like that day when everyone in the kibbutz went to the Rocky Hill (I went because you had insisted that it's important, even though father was against it), and gathered around a stone engraved with the name Micha Oren. And they were all so deathly serious and grim, and their heads hung down as if they were ashamed of something. They wore dark glasses and looked sort of like how blind people look in pictures. And suddenly I had a strong urge to giggle, but I didn't giggle, and didn't even smile because I knew you'd be furious with me, and I wouldn't be able to explain to you that even though I giggled, it wasn't because something funny was going on there. No, I definitely didn't think that things were funny. They were anything but funny. And I saw people's lips move, ever so little, and I didn't understand what they were mumbling, without a voice. And then I heard Old Gara reading from the Bible... Abraham, God called. Yes, Lord, he replied. Take with you your only son, yes, Isaac, whom you love so much, and go to the land of Moriah, and sacrifice him there as a burnt offering upon one of the mountains which I will point out to you.

I didn't believe a word of this horrible story, even when Dahlia, my favorite teacher, read it to us in Bible class. And I hated Abraham, and pitied Isaac, and to my horror, I began to cry in class. The children looked at me with a sort of wonder mixed with mockery, except for Nati, of course, but she too cried a little and pretended she only had the sniffles. And Dahlia caressed my head, and told me to go wash my face and have a drink of water, and not to be so sad because it is only a story. Remember Dahlia, big and soft and very gentle, always raking her hair with chalk-stained fingers, like a plough in a wheat field? And sometimes when I daydreamed of you or watched Nati's legs, Dahlia would stop at my desk and say, Micha, try to concentrate. And I never understood how she knew that I wasn't. The next day, after she read this horrible story to us, you came to school and went with Dahlia to the teacher's room , and you stayed there forever. I hid behind the school among the pomegranates for you to come out, and when you came out, your face was white and worried and your eyes swollen and red, and your legs hardly carried you. And I was sure that you were ill, so I too was worried, and I too was ill, and I vomited among the pomegranate trees. And accordingly I stood behind the school, leaning against its wall, and cried. And you never said a word to me about that meeting, and I never asked. And I knew that you liked Dahlia, because from all the people who wanted to sit with you at lunch or dinner, you always chose to sit with Dahlia, and when I asked you why, you said you had a lot to talk about.

And on that memorial day in the Rocky Hill, oh, Mother, I wanted terribly to run away from there. It was so spooky, and the air hummed with whispers and hisses and echoes, faint cries and sighs. And I was sure that in a moment, evil spirits would attack me, and I longed to hide among the rocks, catch tiny snails, dig for earthworms, and watch how the butterflies tease the flowers. So, I looked down at my feet, and vowed to myself not to think, when suddenly I saw a small turtle, pathetic and helpless, lying on his back on the grass, and feebly flailing its legs in the air in a futile effort to turn over. I wanted to bend down and help him, but I couldn't move because my hand was squeezed inside my father's huge, sweaty palm, and my head swayed. So I looked up at the trees and listened to the birds sing in the branches, and I felt better. And suddenly there was a commotion, people were running toward me. My father dropped my hand, and bending down quickly, I turned the turtle over and whispered, *run away, little turtle, run before they kill you.* And when I looked up, I saw you lying on the grass, and your eyes were closed, and your face was white as chalk, and you looked like a broken doll. And father was kneeling beside you. Then he picked you up and carried you in his arms all the way back to our house. And I ran behind him, and he laid you on the bed and shut the door in my face.

The night of that memorial service, my father sat on my bed for a long time and was very silent. And suddenly I heard myself ask, where do we go after we die? And father said that after death we don't go anywhere. I asked, are you sure? And he said, yes, I'm sure. Who put such absurd ideas in your head? And I insisted that after we die, we meet in heaven, and father sighed and kissed my forehead. His serious eyes were sad and very tired, and I thought I heard him mutter under his breath, Rita, Rita, what are you doing to the child? And he kissed me again. Good night, son, he said. And at that moment I loved him terribly, so I put my arms around his neck, and he hugged me tight to his massive chest, just like I had seen him hug you.

That night, I couldn't fall asleep, and I tossed and turned and counted to a hundred and listened to the frogs and crickets outside and pressed my fingers to my eyes until I saw strange shapes and colors. I even tried to sing under my blanket, but nothing could chase away the dead from the Rocky Hill, and my mind was alert to the slightest move or sound from your bedroom. Maybe you'll come to kiss me good night and hold me tight, and the night will be soft and quiet. Nevertheless in the morning, the sheets were soaked, and the hateful stink of urine greeted the new day, and the cold morning air cut through my wet pajamas. But I hadn't slept all night, so how had it happened? Don't cry; take hold of yourself, I commanded.

The next day, you were unlike yourself. You refused to see your friends and ignored my father, and when you spoke to me, your voice was flat and monotonous. Father left you alone, and your friends shook their heads and clicked their tongues and said, Poor Rita. And I attached myself to you like a leech, and you said, Michal'e, don't you have anything better to do than follow me around all day? You're driving me nuts. But I tugged at your hands and laughed in a tone that even I could tell was most unpleasant, and I told you stories about school and my friends and about Old Gara, who took me to the cow shed to see how a calf is born. So much blood, Mommy, so much blood, but the cow didn't care at all, she licked her baby and licked with a tongue so large and pink and rough, until her baby was smooth and shining. And the calf tripped and fell and got up and again tripped until Old Gera picked him up and put him next to his mother's udder, and the calf sucked and pulled and made funny noises. And Old Gera let me stroke his head, and his head was warm and damp and sticky; so wonderful. And all you said was, Michal'e, don't shout, I'm not deaf Micha, and I got confused because I wasn't aware that I was shouting—well, maybe my voice was a little louder than usual—and I was going to tell you how much I loved Nati, but I didn't because you weren't listening. And I felt as if I were invisible, unnecessary to the world, and I turned away from you, because, at the age of seven, I hadn't understood the meaning of the weird gathering at Rocky Hill, and I knew that Big Micha's body wasn't there because it had been torn to pieces and couldn't be identified. I wished then that I knew what identified meant, and although I wanted to ask many questions, I didn't because every time the words were almost there, my lips got numb and I couldn't utter a sound for fear I wouldn't find the right words.

And I also knew then that before I was born, you wanted to marry Big Micha, because you were in love with him, and I wondered if you had felt about Big Micha the way I felt about Nati. And although this question often occupied my thoughts, I could never really make up my mind about it, because grown-ups, in my opinion, were full of dark secrets, and I felt as though I were living in a place where everyone but me knew an important secret. But no one ever said it out loud, at least not while I was present, not even you.

When did I learn about you and Big Micha? It seemed that I always knew, and I remembered in particular one summer night when the moon was full, and it had been awfully hot and humid. You had left the door to your bedroom wide open, and I was lying awake in my bed, sweating in the sheets, when suddenly I heard you cry and say that you should have married Big Micha. Father answered that Micha wasn't the marrying kind, that he had the soul of a gypsy. I didn't understand, but I shut my eyes tight as if I were waiting for a blow. And then you said something that sounded very strange to me. You don't always marry the one you truly love, was exactly what you'd said, and after that there was silence. And I thought that what you'd said didn't make any sense at all, and that maybe you were even lying, because I loved Nati best of all the girls in the kibbutz, and I was sure that I would marry her as soon as I was through with my army service; perhaps even sooner, because when I thought of Nati, I felt a quiver of pleasure throughout my whole body. Nati's legs were beautiful, and her hair had the color of your hair, and her eyes were huge and brown and almond shaped, and I had no doubt then that I was going to marry her. And later in that night, I heard you say, *I shouldn't have given in to his romantic talk about living together. Rita, he would say, what difference does it make what people say? But it made a difference to me, and I shouldn't have listened to him, especially after I learned about my condition.* Rita, Rita, father cajoled, it's enough. I'm begging you, it's enough. But you only laughed a terrible laugh, or maybe you were crying. And I didn't hear any more because I jammed my fingers into my ears, and saw the walls of my room moving, closing in on me. At that moment, Mother, I hated you. And in my dream that night, I was crushing Big Micha's skull with a big stone, and I smashed and smashed. But his skull wouldn't break, and his mouth whispered something I didn't understand, and I raised the stone to strike again, but instead of a stone, my hand was gripping a hand, and the hand was your hand. I woke up terrified and crying, and you came running from your room and got into my bed and gathered my body into your arms and didn't seem to mind the stench of urine. I clung to you and sobbed, Mommy, I had a bad dream. And you said in a soft voice, It's all right, grown-ups have bad dreams too. Hush, my darling, I am here now. You don't have to be afraid anymore. There are no bad dreams now; hush. You cuddled me to your body and sang to me in your small, sad voice, song after song, and you made my fear melt away. I fell asleep pressing my face into your breasts.

And I hated to be called Little Micha. I was the tallest in my class, and every time I passed the hall mirror, I saw a broad-shouldered boy with tight red curls and a freckled face that I detested, but which grown-ups thought cute. My one consolation was my eyes, green, like yours. Big Micha's eyes, I was told, were brown like my father's because it's natural for brothers to have the same eye color. But most of all, I hated my hair. I hated it so much that one day, when I came back from school, I went straight to the kitchen cabinet where you kept a bottle of olive oil and emptied the entire contents on my head, and when I looked in the bathroom mirror, I clapped my hands and shouted, Magic! Magic! because my curly hair turned straight and brown like my father's. But the olive oil dripped into my eyes, and I rubbed my eyelids with my fists, and the world looked like a messy jigsaw puzzle. And then I saw you standing at the door (I hadn't even heard you come home) and pretended to ignore you, but in my heart, I wondered why you hadn't said anything or got angry. You only watched me silently, your face whiter than usual. Finally, almost blind and the olive oil burning in my eyes, I went to you for help. And you didn't say a word, you only took me by the hand back to the bathroom and washed my head and rinsed my eyes. And then I was standing between your knees while you rubbed my head with a towel until it felt as if the skin of my scalp were coming off together with my hateful hair. And you cupped my face between the palms of your hands, and your eyes were two green stars, and you said, Michal'e, this is the way God had made you. It's important to like yourself as you are. But I insisted angrily, I want to look like my father. And you rose from the chair, still holding my face between the palms of your hands, and said, King David had red hair, and he was the most handsome man in the Bible. I felt my anger rising and pulled away from you; while tears were choking my throat, I screamed at you that I didn't care about King David's hair and that your hair wasn't red either. At that moment, you were standing with your back against the window, and the afternoon sun was behind you, and its yellow rays were making your hair gold. And I said, Like sunlight, your hair is like sunlight. Only mine is red. Disgusting! And I saw the green of your eyes turning hard and gray and your hands left my cheeks, and you said, You're lucky to have red hair. Big Micha had red hair, and he was as beautiful as King David. At that moment, I knew that he will always be between us. Big Micha is dead! I shouted in your face. Dead people are not lucky. Their bodies get torn to pieces, and no one knows where they're buried. That's what happens to people with red hair. And I saw how you almost stopped breathing and your face blanched, and for a moment, you stood there speechless. Then you whispered, My god, what are you saying? And I screamed, Old Gara said that it brings bad luck to name a boy after his dead uncle. I heard him say so. I heard him say it many times, to many people. I heard him say it to my father! And your face turned this awful shade of purple red, and you raised your hand. And for the first time in my life, I was sure you were going to hit me across the face, and I stuck my head between my shoulders, waiting for the blow, but you lowered your hand.

Gera, you spat his name, I should have known, the old fool. You shouldn't listen to what people say. I don't listen! I screamed. I hear. I hear them whisper. They whisper all the time! And you grabbed me by the shoulders, and my eyes, open to their limits, were in your eyes, and my anger choked me. A weird smile hovered on your face, and you said, Big Micha was a wonderful man, and you let go of my shoulders, and I released my breath and let go of your eyes. You said in your soft, sad voice, my beautiful man. And you touched my hair, but your gaze was far away, and your eyes were full of longing. I swallowed my tears, tensed my body, and thought in my heart, no, I'm not a baby. I didn't cling or cry—as long as I could help it. And so I turned away from you, and stuck my hands in my pockets and went to play with my friends. But on the way, I threw a few stones at Sam the Cat, and scored a point this time. Sam ran away, howling like mad, but I didn't feel triumphant. I only walked aimlessly along the narrow path, hitting the shrubs and kicking the stones and praying not to be seen by anyone. And I thought to myself that you said many things I didn't understand, and I wanted so much to be sure they were good things, because your voice was soft and your face so pretty, but I loved your eyes above all. They were green and clear, and, at times, kind of blue or grey. And sometimes I would catch you looking strangely, and your gaze would be focused on something I couldn't see, something beyond my head, and you would be smiling this special, longing smile. Then I would run to you, put my arms around your waist, and press my face into your belly, longing to tell you not to be sad, Mama, because I love you and I'd take care of you. And you would caress my hair, and your touch would send waves and tingles throughout my entire body, and you would say you loved me more than anyone else in the whole world. Then why would I feel that you were talking to someone who wasn't there, Mother,

Mother? And you never called me Little Micha. You called me Michal'e, and I wondered if it was because you knew how mad it made me to be called Little Micha. It drove me insane when someone would ruffle my hair and pinch my cheek and say Big Micha all the way. The eyes are Rita's, still, a spitting image. Big Micha was a brave man. You're brave too, right?

At moments like that, I would feel my anger consuming me like a fire. My breathing would stop, and I would stand frozen. My hands would curl into tight fists ready to punch and do something really nasty, like I did that day when, after school, I went to the cowshed where old Gara worked. I liked going to the cowshed in the winter, but you would grumble and pull a face and say, don't come near me, Michal'e. You stink like a cow. Again you went to the cowshed? What are you looking for there? Why don't you play with friends? But I didn't care if I stunk like a cow. It was friendly there, and warm and smelly and dirty and steamy, and Old Gera would let me drink milk right from the cow's udder. I never told you that because I knew you'd be annoyed and preach to me for days about viruses, bacteria, and health. Sometimes Old Gara would tell me jokes I didn't understand, like the joke about the farmer and his cow, and something about love and tits, and when I asked him, what's tits, that knocked Old Gara out. He began to laugh like a madman and collapsed onto the milking bench. I was afraid he'd die laughing, and suddenly I found myself laughing and mooing, like I had never laughed and mooed, until my stomach hurt, and tears rolled down my cheeks. Oh, Mother, it felt wonderful. So what if I hadn't understood the joke? And I was still laughing and mooing and jumping about the barn when suddenly I noticed Old Gara glaring at me, as if I'd stolen something. So I stopped dancing, and cocked my head and asked, what? And Old Gara said, They ought to tell you. It isn't right. You look exactly like him. And why not. It's absolutely normal for a boy to look like his . . . The rest of the words hung over me like dirty laundry, and my heart began to pound, and the blood rushed to my face. I screamed, I look like my father! Then I bent down and stuck my hand in a manure pile and picked up a handful of cow shit and threw it in Gara's face. I ran out of the cowshed and hid in the granary. And there, in the granary, surrounded by whispers, I had a huge asthma attack, and I spun for hours on a white cloud.

In the evening, when Father asked how I could behave in such a disgusting manner, I glared into his eyes and remained silent. What could I say; tell him about the rage, the despair, the whispers, the double-meaning glances that are thrown at me? Why, Michal'e; why, you pleaded? I wanted to run to you and scream, love me like you love Big Micha, but I couldn't. I felt like a rag was stuffed into my throat, and I couldn't even whisper. That evening, I received my first thrashing from my father, and you sat watching, not saying a word. But your eyes were full of tears.—like the stones on Rocky Hill—and wounded, and your hands were tightly clenched in your lap. During the beating, I felt nothing.

Later that same night, when you thought I was asleep, I heard my father say, I think we should tell him. It's better for the kid to know. You shouted, no! And Father asked, When, Rita? And you said, your voice full of dread, not yet, he's too young. He won't understand. {Did you really think that I didn't understand? You were very naive, Mama.} And Father said, It's time, Rita. He isn't a baby anymore. And you began to cry. No, Eli. God no. He'll never forgive me. He even hates his own name, and he'll hate me. {How is it possible that you hadn't known, Mama, that I could never hate you? How could you disappear like that, betray me, let me grow up without you, have a bar mitzvah without you, go into the army to become a paratrooper without you?}

And Father said, and his voice came from somewhere deep inside his belly, Rita, Rita, what am I going to do with you? And that night, when I was waiting for sleep to come and take me, I thought to myself that maybe it's better after all to be an orphan, like this boy Copperfield you'd been reading to me about. So strong was the image of being without you stamped upon my mind that I jumped up and threw away the red blanket and shouted, NO! I ran to the window, and for a moment, I stood there rooted to the floor and shut my eyes tight and listened with all my might. Yes, I shouted, and clapped my hands and flung the window open, and realized that the storm had blown itself out, and the silence was as complete as if God had turned the whole world off.

I stayed by the open window for a while and sniffed the wetness and savored the stillness, and then I went to your bedroom, and I sat on your bed, and my eyes fell on the picture of the soldier with the red hair and found myself face-to-face with my own smile. And with my eyes locked on the picture, I squeezed my body under your blanket and hid my face in your pillow and hissed venomously at the man in the picture, I'm glad you're dead; I hate you. I hate you. But the truth was I didn't feel hatred for anyone, and the silence was soothing, and I was so tired, and soon the buzz in my head became vague, as if it came from a great distance or belonged to someone else. And I turned my face to the wall and squirmed deeper under the blanket where it was dark and warm and smelt like your body and hair, and my eyes closed with pleasure. Suddenly I heard a noise. Someone was coming. I bolted out of the bed and was running. Mommy! Mommy! I shouted, and clapped my hands. I jerked the door wide open. But it wasn't you who was standing there, smiling. I promised, didn't I, said my little friend, Nati, and walked right past me into the living room. Why are you wearing pajamas, Michal'e, she asked? Are you ill? I didn't answer. I only gazed at her as if she were a miracle. I saw a million snails and earthworms by the dining hall, Nati said. Really, I said, and caught my breath, feeling the shreds of the storm in my head retreating, backing off, as if being chased away by this little bit of a girl. Wonderful puddles, Nati said, everywhere. Her huge, brilliant, almond-shaped eyes were fixed on my face, urging, teasing, and I knew she was up to something mischievous. I looked away from her, down at the floor and said, I was scared of the storm. And she said, Me too. I looked at her and asked, You really were afraid? And she said, Aha. And I watched how the rain dripped from her hair onto her eyelashes, onto her shoulders, onto her blouse, onto her shoes, onto every part of her body, and rainwater ran down her legs into the floor. She was sucking out the moisture from a bunch of hair between her lips, and my body relaxed, and I laughed. You're lying, you love storms, you told me so yourself. But she ignored my words and said, you know, Michal'e, I saw a turtle on the way, and I asked, a big turtle? She chuckled, So-so, and suddenly we were laughing and jumping and shouting, and making a big wet mess on your spotless carpet. And I felt my pajama bottom slipping down my legs toward the floor, and I caught it just in time. And that's how we were when you came home.

Out of the corner of my eye, I saw you standing at the open door, watching. Your eyes were their deepest green, and you said in your soft, sad voice, Michal'e, my beautiful boy, and my heart leaped with joy.

How did you leave me, Mother? How did you leave me? You pointed the rifle toward your heart and squeezed the trigger. Didn't you know that you were everything, and everything in me goes back to you? They say it was an accident, they say you didn't know the gun was loaded. What do they really know about you? And they're still whispering . . . always whispering.

It seems to me that sorrow has no voice, I think to myself: where were your arms when I was still twined in webs of dream, when I stretched out to you tiny arms in primordial thirst? And you: you turned away your head and closed the door behind your back; I didn't know yet how to cry your name. For years I wandered in the fields, gathering dry leaves, breathing the scent of decaying flowers. The anemones froze; the daffodils emitted an evil laugh. You were harsh as a fruitless soil. Now you are dead and I am still searching for you, lost, among shadows of frozen anemones…

CHAPTER 17

Aliya

OH READER, I THINK ABOUT OUR EXCITEMENT at that time; it was a different sort, weaving inside, weaving slowly, knitting a carpet of utopia. An excited anticipation of the stirring presence, and sun, so much sun. Even so, it was an excitement of a different sort, not gut-wrenching, not hilarious, quiet, with a long breath. Through lemon orchards, through inflamed sunrises we did not go in vain. Even though our faces were lifted to heaven and stars flickered in our eyes, we knew that the desert of bones lay only a few steps from us.

I am tired. What more can I demand from time? Another toxin? spiritual marijuana? I will stay right here, until you tell me otherwise; and you, my childhood friends? Please look for me. The heart of the woods pervades my thoughts and I am taken back to a time when red, red anemones were in bloom, alongside a military presence. Yes, sorry, I forgot to tell you about the war and the way people in the kibbutz handled it. It isn't easy to narrate. I was 13 years old during the war of independence in Israel.

We were bombed from the air regularly; machine guns deafened our ears, grenades blew up next to us. We did not have shelters; we were huddled together in trenches and counted the bombs. Every few minutes our principal from school came to the trench, his clothes spotted with fresh blood. He came to tell us who was killed, that day, who wounded. We were not afraid at the time of the wars. The fear came much later in life. In the story I wrote here, I concentrate on what happened to certain people after the war. It is a true story; only the names are different. Here it is:

{For the E-Book version place a link here to the video, Anemones, by John Brusseau}

And when the silence was at its deepest, the stillness so complete and undisturbed that even the crickets ceased their shouting, the watchman on duty was dozing off somewhere, Alya arose from her bed as if obeying a command, and dressed in her nightclothes, went to the door and opened it. For a long moment, she stood at the open door listening, then closed the door behind her and walked into the night. The way she walked was more like floating, down the moonlit path, straight toward the old water tower where a month earlier, wrapped in blood-stained army blankets, five corpses had lain on the ground.

Five dead soldiers. She sang softly, I am dreaming, and my eyes can see . . . Anemones, red, red anemones . . .

Time leaped back. Again she saw them, lying in a straight line, their naked feet sticking out of the bloody blankets. She bent down and, one after the other, lifted the blankets and searched the faces with the tips of her fingers, softly touched the faces. But he wasn't among them. Gill she called! Gill! And she began walking around the dead soldiers just as she had walked then—that day, during the war, the day they'd brought the bodies. Red, red anemones, she sang until she heard Gill's voice, and his voice was soft and clear and bright.

Tomorrow will be a beautiful day. Go to the woods. To our secret place.

Yes, she said. Yes. Tomorrow... in the woods. Our secret place. Yes, listen Gill; I've something important to tell you . . . But Gill was gone, the dead soldiers vanished, she alone was standing by the old water tower, smiling at nothing. And still singing Gill's favorite tune, she returned to her room. She went on singing, even softer, as she got back into her bed. For a while, she lay quietly, her eyes wide-open; she remembered the sky that seemed almost black, each star a burning flame, the moon bigger and brighter than she'd ever seen it, the moss that sprouted out of the cracks in the cement of the old water tower, the smell of death on the soldiers' faces as she leaned close to touch them. Then the night around her softened, and only Gill's gentle voice lingered in her mind, lulling her to sleep.

And while Alya slept a dreamless sleep, in another bed in the same room, Orna pulled the covers over her head, her brain alert and restless, though her body lay rigid and still. The fear she came face-to-face with every night, when Alya left the room, did not end when Alya returned, and in order to bring sleep, Orna closed her eyes, longing to dive into the realm of dreams, to evolve toward another more satisfying form of existence. And she fastened her mind on the happy memories of her childhood, before the war.

And while Alya slept and Orna conjured up pictures of happy, carefree days, in the bed under the window, Ruthie turned toward the wall, beset by ominous thoughts: How long was this lunacy going to go on? Weren't they going to do something about Alya? The war was over. Why don't they do something? Tears of frustration wet her pillow as she lay there in the suffocating stillness, yearning to sleep.

On Saturday afternoon, Orna was sitting on the lawn in a spot of brilliant sunlight, lost in gloomy thoughts, as she leafed abstractedly through a small book of poetry. Her head ached, her temple throbbed, her eyelids were sore and slightly puffy after a night of troubled sleep. She let the book drop to the grass, closed her eyes, and abandoned herself to the consoling warmth of the afternoon sun. Her face relaxed a little. From one of the houses, she heard faint singing. *Red, red anemones . . .*

She sat motionless while the song lasted. When it stopped, she opened her eyes and raised her head. Suddenly she noticed Alya slinking like a tomcat between trees and shrubberies, careful to avoid meeting anyone. Perhaps Orna knew what her friend was up to. Perhaps she didn't. But she leapt to her feet and called, Alya! And she watched as her friend halted abruptly, then turned and slowly came across the grass towards her.

Well, Orna said, why are you sneaking around like a criminal? I am going to the woods, said Alya. Orna felt her heart lurch in her chest. You can't be serious, she said in a fierce whisper, fixing her blue eyes wide-open upon Alya. Why not? I love the woods. Orna, striving to keep her voice even, said, I love the woods too, but I don't go there. Alya smiled enigmatically. That's because you don't have a soul. What do you mean I don't have a soul? Oh, never mind; you and your fancy words. Orna leaned forward, her face almost touching Alya's. Tell me, she breathed. You might as well tell me because I saw you talking to him, alone. Orna felt like punching Alya—actually, all day she had felt like punching someone, anyone.

I'm meeting Ari in the woods at five o'clock, said Alya. Orna lost her cool altogether. Are you mad? You don't even know him. I know him, said Alya. He's nice. He's a poet. So, He's old. I hear he's twenty, maybe even more. Orna, feeling helplessly annoyed, glared at her friend. What's wrong with you anyway? Don't you ever read the paper? Orna, you're in love with him. Alya's voice was low and even. I'm not. Orna made a desperate effort to sound nonchalant. Oh, muttered Alya. Oh what? Orna barked at her friend. I'm glad you're not in love with him, that's all, said Alya, her voice slightly apologetic.

Orna stared at her friend, her blue eyes wild. No, she concluded to herself, she's definitely nothing special to look at. She looks ten, not fifteen, and she doesn't even have boobs. She's so skinny. Orna took a deep breath, deliberately extending her well-developed breasts. Thank God I don't have freckles and red hair, she thought, and with a flick of her head, tossed her long yellow hair, then noticed that Alya's eyes were fixed upon her face with a sort of an innocent yet mischievous glint, and that her lips parted slightly in a little smile. Yes, Orna thought, it's this innocent look in her eyes, this smile. She recalled Ruthie telling her the other day that people were talking about how strange Alya had become.

The last rumor, Ruthie had said with a weird look of excitement on her plump baby face, is that at night, Alya has been seen walking near that awful place by the old water tower where the dead soldiers were laid, talking and singing to herself and calling her father's name. And I heard people say, if this continues, something drastic should be done.

Orna, determined in her loyalty to Alya, immediately jumped to her friend's defense. This is a vicious rumor. Alya sleeps in the same room with you and me, and I've never seen her leave in the middle of the night, or talk to herself. And as far as calling out her father's name—honestly, Ruthie, sometimes you make me sick. Don't you understand anything? You know it's true, Ruthie had said. Every night you wait for her to return from the old water tower; every night. And even after she returns, you can't sleep, and neither can I. So don't pretend you don't know.

Yes, of course, Orna knew. Everyone knew. Now, looking at Alya's upturned face, Orna thought how changed Alya was by her father's death. Not that she was ever ordinary; everything about her was a little eccentric, out of accord with the rest of her friends. But as time passed, it had become more and more apparent that Alya no longer inhabited their world, that she lived in a private world of her own, where all dimension seemed to be eliminated between the living and the dead, a mysterious world that belongs only to her and her father, Gill. And when people mentioned the war or talked of death, a hard and remote expression would invade Alya's face, leaving her brilliant brown eyes expressionless. And she would walk way. And Orna would watch her with anxious heart, a tide of pain rising to her chest, and she would follow her friend and walk by her side, and silently watch Alya's pale, almost luminous, face. And she would swallow her tears.

And of course, everyone talked about the war—that was all they talked about. So more often than not, instead of going to school, Alya would go to the woods or the olive grove, sit under a tree, and read; mostly dream. And sometimes Orna would find her fast asleep with her face buried in a bunch of yellow dandelions that grew in abundance under the trees. Alya would say that school was boring, that she was so happy in the woods and the grove. Don't tell on me, Orna. Please don't tell on me, she would plead. So if anyone asked her if she knew where Alya was, Orna would merely shrug her shoulders and say impatiently, What am I, her guardian? How should I know? And yet Alya's growing remoteness was something very difficult for Orna to bear.

And now Alya was going to the woods to meet this stranger, Ari, the new poetry teacher. Alya, Orna said, sadness mingled with impatience replacing her anger, don't you know it's dangerous to go to the woods? Dangerous? Why? Why? Why do you think there are still so many soldiers there? And what about the mines? Don't you remember when Boaz stepped on a mine and everyone in the kibbutz was sure he would die? Gill said Boaz wouldn't die. Alya smiled serenely. Gill knows everything. Orna wanted to scream that Gill was dead, that he was killed in the war and would never come back. But she merely looked at the ground and viciously kicked at the grass with the toe of her shoe.

You have a morbid mind, Orna, Alya said. You make up all kinds of stories. You see demons and evil spirits everywhere—you scare yourself crazy. And you're always confusing things. It's true that Boaz stepped on a mine, but it didn't happen in the woods, it happened near the cornfield. The papers... I don't read the papers. Besides, Ari will be there to protect me. How? Does he have a gun? Orna was rapidly losing her temper again. But Alya merely smiled. No, she said gently. He doesn't have a gun. He has a book of poetry.

Orna leaned forward a little and, glaring straight into Alya's eyes, said, He's so odd and so silent. You shouldn't be alone with him. Did you see the scar on his cheek? Ruthie told me that during the war, he was with the commando unit in the Arava desert and got wounded in the face by a shrapnel. Ruthie also said that he never talks about the war because he saw terrible things happen there, and that— for three months after he got wounded—he didn't talk at all, and that he himself almost got killed, and— Orna clamped a hand over her mouth, letting out a low sound, as she saw the familiar empty look in Alya's eyes; and as her friend turned away from her, she grabbed her hand. Alya, she groaned, I'm sorry. Alya turned back to face her friend. She stood silent, her face white and remote and detached, her eyes turned inward. I have to go now, she said after a moment and walked away. Alya! Wait! Orna called, sobbing.

Alya walked toward the gate of the kibbutz. Amos, her dog, trotted beside her, licking her hand. His damp black eyes were begging for her attention, but his efforts were not being rewarded as usual. Go home, Amos, Alya said. The dog fixed accusing, hurt eyes on her and whined mournfully. Then he laid back his ears, turned around, and crouched at the kibbutz gate to wait.

Outside the gate of the kibbutz, Alya began to run. It was two miles from the kibbutz to the woods, and the world around her glistened green, pure and tranquil. The old eucalyptuses on each side of the road rushed past her as if moving backward. She ran fast, trying not to think. But it was no use. She couldn't stop the incessant chatter of her mind. She was remembering how, when, after poetry class on Friday, Ari had stopped her and asked if she could meet him somewhere—anywhere; she should only name the place—on Saturday at five. He took her by such surprise that for a moment she merely stood gaping at him, then flushed, her mind twisting with confusion. Why me? but he said with an encouraging smile: to read poetry. She looked at him closely, and noticed two bitter-looking lines around his mouth. His hair was black and curly, his face narrow and dark, and his lips full. A red scar in the shape of a rose was etched high on his right cheekbone. But it was his eyes that touched her imagination: deep-set black eyes that looked at her with gentleness and appreciation. Perhaps the way Gill's eyes looked at her. I like him, she thought.

To read poetry? She paused. Okay. Where should we meet?

Go to the woods. To our regular place, says Gill.

In the woods, came out of her mouth like in a dream, by the Kissing Stone. The Kissing Stone? She blushed, giggled nervously, and bit her lips. It's only a name of a big white rock in the woods. He said nothing, only looked at her with his head tilted, and she saw fine, hardly visible lines creasing the corners of his eyes. Well, she said, with a sort of daring shyness, it's only a rock. When our parents lived inside the woods, they named it the Kissing Stone. I didn't know the kibbutz was built inside the woods. There are many things about us you don't know.

He smiled at her good-humoredly. But I'm learning fast. Why did they move from the woods to the hill? They had to. Living in the woods wasn't safe then because—oh, I don't remember that time, I was only a little girl. Anyway, the Kissing Stone is easy to sit on, and you can't miss it because it's the biggest rock in the woods, and it's very, very white.

She looked around, uneasy at being seen with him alone. People talk. Oh never mind, she thought. Let them talk; they would anyhow. And when he said, I hear the woods aren't exactly a safe place now either, she pulled herself up and looked defiantly into his eye, challenging. It's safe enough, she said. I go there all the time. Then a small devil leapt inside her, and a little mischievous smile lifted the corners of her mouth. She said, except of course for the snakes. She saw the look in his eyes change. Big snakes, he asked; his voice soft but subtle, stroking her nerves like balm. She whispered, enormous, and watching him laugh, she laughed with him. But the moment was a difficult one for her; perhaps for him too.

Now, reviewing the entire scene, each detail fresh and alive, Alya felt hot and sticky. Not quite real. He had chosen her, and she wondered how a thing like that could have happened to her. If I were him, she was thinking, I would have chosen Orna. Orna is so sophisticated, adventurous, and of course, the prettiest.

My beautiful girl. My clever little honeybee, says Gill.

Near the woods, Alya slackened her pace. Her legs felt strange as though her knees were made of gum. Her red hair stuck to her flushed, damp cheeks, and her shirt was soaking wet. Is that what Gill means when he talks about love? she wondered. At that moment, she wished Amos, her dog, was with her, or even Orna. Oh, don't panic. It'll be all right, she admonished herself.

When she reached the edge of the woods, she stopped running and stood to listen. She listened, not only with her ears, but also with her whole person, her face assuming an odd, mystical expression. After a moment, she took off her shoes and slowly entered the woods. The stillness was complete and soothing, stroking her nerves like a mother's gentle hand. The damp pine needles yielded, submissive and soft, under the light pressure of her bare feet, and a red winter sun, acting as a chaperone, winked at her through the branches of the trees. The ground was crimson with anemones. She sang softly, *Red, red anemones . . .*

She picked an anemone and slightly caressed her face with its delicate petal, inhaling the fresh, poignant fragrance of recent rain and pine needles. She walked slowly, feeling the warmth of the sun on her back and shoulders, when suddenly the stillness was interrupted by a loud, abrupt metallic sound. She turned quickly, but saw nothing unusual: only dense blankets of scarlet, white, and yellow flowers beneath the tall grass under the trees. The wild thumping of her heart subsided. She sighed and shrugged; then, singing, entered the long, narrow avenue of cypresses. After a while, she turned to the right where the pine branches entwined, converging into an awning to shade her head. With the anemone's flowers, she wove a red laurel with which she adorned her head and forehead, securing it with hairpins. A slight breeze began to stir. She saw the cypress tops sway gently. Sparrows, wagtails, bulbuls and red-breasted robins sang all around her. Then she saw the Kissing Stone, solid as ever. And there was Ari, sitting on its flat surface, reading from a small book.

Dazed with excitement, Alya became, almost unconscious of her surroundings, a little frightened. Holding her breath, she crept closer and watched him from behind the gnarled trunk of an old acacia tree. She thought him beautiful. Suddenly he got up and began to recite. She couldn't hear the words he uttered; his voice was only a murmur. But his face was entirely visible to her and she saw him grimace, and gesture wildly like a mad actor on an invisible stage. She giggled. He looked around. Alya? She crouched lower behind the tree's trunk. She saw him look at his watch. She looked at hers. Five o'clock. She stood still, listening again, completely absorbed.

Here I come, she said, and from among the shadows of the trees, she stepped out into the bright light of the clearing. With the red laurel on her head, she walked bravely to meet him.

He turned and saw her standing with her shoes in her hand, her feet bare and mud-caked, and the red-anemone laurel circling her head like little leaping flames. He gazed at her, enchanted, his face white and tense, his right hand clutching the book of poetry to his chest. She looked so young and timid it scared him, made him feel uncertain of himself. The reality of their situation suddenly confused him. What were his intentions toward her?

From the first moment he had seen her, she dominated his thoughts. He wished to be alone with her, to know her. And yet as much as he was attracted to her, something about her disturbed him, made him feel perplexed. She was completely different from anyone he'd ever met. She seemed always to be mocking a little. Not overtly, not obviously, and definitely not with malice; but it was there in the glint of her eyes, in her smile. Her smile—the most charming smile he had ever seen on a human face yet—also most disquieting. A smile that was ironic and sweet, innocent, yet knowing: pure joy and passion mixed with deep sorrow. And still he felt compelled to know her.

Alya, you're really here? he said softly, trying to hide his confusion. Yes, she laughed. Not knowing what else to say, he asked, Did you see the soldiers? No, she said, and he saw her body stiffen. He looked at her in wonder. She liked his shyness. It made him seem younger, and it made her feel older, a little bolder. But she wasn't going to talk about wars or death, and she hoped he wasn't going to talk about them either. She wouldn't be able to bear it. She would have to walk away from him, and she didn't want to walk away from him.

I like him, she thought. His eyes are so gentle. She stood meditating, and looked deep into the shade of the dense foliage, listening to the songs of the insects in the grass. She was conscious of his eyes upon her and his silence. She hesitated a moment; then, with a small frown on her face, said, The woods seem somehow different.

Different? he asked. How? The woods seem so calm today as if hiding an important secret. Orna would say, It is full of demons and spirits. She giggled, embarrassed at her own words. Probably because of the soldiers, he said; they seem to be everywhere.

She said nothing but looked at him intently, her face pale, her eyes pained. Suddenly she felt trapped in her loneliness, lost inside herself, and, as if she were cold, she hugged her shoulders.

Only a bad dream. Shah . . . , says Gill.

Perhaps at that moment, as she met his eyes, and he saw the terrible pain in them, Ari began to understand, to know her. He reached out his hand as if to wipe the fear off her heart. She looked at him, transfixed. His fingers touched her cheek. She shut her eyes. She felt as if she wanted to hide herself in him, in his gentleness, in his strength. She opened her eyes.

Shah . . . Nothing to be afraid of. I'm here, says Gill.

She sat on the stone's surface, her head turned toward the setting sun, her eyes squinting at the early-evening radiance. For a while, they sat in silence—she looking at the sky, he looking at her. Then she turned to him and said, this stone means so much to so many. And with the open palm of her right hand, she slowly, sensually caressed the stone. Perhaps she was thinking about his hand on her face.

Tell me about it. He took her hands and held them for a moment between his. It means happiness and disappointment, dreams and love and—death. When our parents were young, they used to meet here. She blushed. Oh, she said in a little voice, I don't really know how to talk about it. It's our parents' secret. And suddenly she felt foolish, sitting like that in the exposed clearing with the red anemone laurel on her head and her hands held in his. But her hands felt right and comfortable in his. Perhaps more. The blush deepened on her cheeks.

Let's read poetry, Ari said. He jumped off the stone, pulling her with him, spread a blanket on the damp grass, and sat upon it. She sat next to him, her shoulder barely touching his. She removed the hairpins from the red laurel and let it slide down, around her neck. As she leaned back against the Kissing Stone, her fear disappeared. She felt safe again. Safe with him. He opened his book of poetry and read to her simply, his voice rich. She closed her eyes and tipped her head back until it rested on the stone, listening to the poet's words and the man's voice. At that moment she felt in harmony with the red sun and the tranquil universe.

And when you're completely silent, you'll hear the wings of the butterflies, says Gill.

Ari closed the book and quietly looked at her. How beautiful. She smiled. Poetry; Gill loves poetry. Gill? He looked at her questioningly. For a moment she looked at him in silence, as if not sure that she wanted to tell him. Gill is my father, she said in a quiet, soft voice. The people in the kibbutz say he was killed in the war by a bullet. But to me he's alive. He's always with me. He talks to me. People think I'm mad, and perhaps they are right, but I have no choice. You'd like Gill. You're like him, a little. Would you like to know him? Yes, Ari said. Slowly she withdrew her hands from his. She sat completely still with only a smile on her lips; and her brown eyes, full of light and shadow, gazed at the sky with a sort of rapture. Perhaps she was hearing Gill's voice at that moment.

She spoke very softly; Gill and I come here every day in winter. Gill talks to me about the butterflies and the birds and the flowers and trees and of all the earth's creatures. Gill and I, we have a bond between us. Gill never says, go to school, Alya. You've got to be like everyone else, Alya. He says, come, the vineyards are heavy with grapes, the orchards laden with fruit. Come let us go for a heavenly walk. That's the way Gill talks. And we walk in the fall, and in winter, and we walk in the spring, and in summer. And we walk for hours. And Gill always hums a tune to himself, and his voice is joyful, his eyes are full of light, and always laughing. Gill's eyes are green, and his hair is red and thick and curly and coarse like lamb's wool. When Rina, my mother, wants to tease him, she says he looks like a broom caught on fire, but to me he looks like a pillar of light.

Sometimes Rina would join us on our walks, but not very often, because she isn't very strong. She is delicate, and tires quickly. But then Rina doesn't care for the vineyards and orchards and woods the way Gill and I do. She says, it's awfully hot and sticky there, and that there are millions of bees and wasps and all kinds of dangerous creatures living among the grapes, peaches, apples, and flowers. Once, in the vineyard, I was stung by a wasp, and my face was swollen for days; my eyes disappeared altogether. I looked so ugly, just like I did when I had the mumps. Gill called me a chipmunk, and said it wasn't so bad, it would toughen me up. But Rina was terribly upset, and fussed over me as if I were in grave danger. I loved being fussed over like that by Rina. Gill kept teasing her and quoting to her from the Bible, saying that like the Shulamit, she was fairest among women. And he called her his lily of the valley, and he took her in his arms and kissed her until she stopped talking. And I saw her burrow her face in his woolly coarse red hair; and in his hair, she later told me, she smelled the fields and the earth and the air. And he made her forget all that existed outside their unity, and that was very nice, and made me very happy. Rina and Gill are crazy about each other, and Gill once told me that he kissed Rina for the first time right here on the Kissing Stone. Rina says that Gill and I are birds of a feather, and that we'll be the death of her, we're so wild. I wish Rina could feel him like I do. But she doesn't. And she has that funny look on her face when I say that he is only lost somewhere, and she has to find him; then it won't hurt so much, and she won't feel so lonely. She looks at me, and a strange smile appears on her face, and I can tell that she doesn't see me at all. Perhaps she sees Gill. I don't really know. And she begins to cry silently and pulls me to her and kisses me all over my face, and her tears wet my face, and she moans and sighs so sadly I want to run away. It's unbearable.

Alya looked at Ari. Have you ever met her? Ari didn't answer. He was sitting erect, his body utterly still, as though held by a terrible tension; and his face, she saw, was suddenly distorted as if he were gripped by an intolerable pain.

Ari wiped the sweat from his brow. Someone, or was it something, was laughing at him with a piercing shriek. Shells whistled around him. The jeep he was driving blew right from under him. Three of his friends were torn to pieces. He pressed his open palm to the wound in Dan's throat. He was drenched in Dan's blood; the taste of it was in his mouth. He was breathing blood; blood was on his face, on his hands, in his eyes. Dan! he screamed. Dan! Don't die! But Dan, his best friend, was dead. He stopped breathing just like that. The terrible rage of that moment threatened once more to obliterate his sanity. He felt the nausea rising up in him. The ghastly, helpless feeling was with him. In him. He was in agony, and was unable for a moment to collect himself.

His mind was still locked on the image of his dying friend, when he felt a pressure on his hand. And when he turned his head and looked at Alya, he was looking out of his chaos down into her uplifted, faintly flushed face and vivid brown eyes. Gill says pain is only an illusion, she said. And Gill once told me that the Bushmen of the Kalahari Desert say there is a dream always dreaming us. Then she smiled and removed the red anemone laurel from around her neck, and crouching on her knees, she slowly placed it at the edge of the blanket, for Gill. She hesitated a moment, then turned her head and looked at him. You understand, don't you? About Gill, I mean.

Yes, he knew. He understood. She lived inside her imagination. She was chained to the ghost of her dead father as he was chained to the ghost of his slain friend. And for one breathless moment, he imagined himself setting her free, bearing her away, saving her. Suddenly he imagined the man, Gill, shot through the chest, lying on the arid ground of the Arava desert with the hot wind roughing his flame-like hair, his eyes open into a blue and empty heaven. Ari clenched his fists. And as if she were reading his thoughts, he heard her whisper, If I let go of Gill now, I'll lose him forever. Yes, he said. They looked at each other. Pained. He took her hand again. They sat in silence, and listened to their ghosts as they watched the winter sun bleeding its dying rays over the branches of the trees.

The moment Alya disappeared from her sight, Orna went quickly to the room she shared with her and Ruthie. She put on an old pair of sneakers, and a white sweater over her blouse, and tied a scarf around her blond curls. Suddenly she sat down on her bed, and stared in front of her as if under a spell, her heart boiling with raging and conflicting emotions. Of course she was jealous of Ari being sweet on Alya and not on her, but she also knew that wasn't what made her feel so utterly devastated. She couldn't understand the restlessness that came upon her with such a force. She felt bewildered, afraid, and unbearably sad. Oh, she cried and banged her fists on the bed. One day, I'll go away... far, far away. Away from hate, from wars, from death. She kept hitting the bed with her clenched fist until her hands were raw. She felt no relief. She thought of another conversation she had with Ruthie: Ruthie had said, this Alya, she's always up to something weird, like going to the woods where no one goes now. And the way she talks about her father; real freaky. She seems to be the only one in the kibbutz who doesn't know that he's dead. And the way she never cries; never. She didn't cry the day they told her he was dead; she didn't shed a tear at his funeral... not a tear. You saw how she was. You stood at her side as they lowered him into the ground. You never took your eyes off her, and you didn't cry either. I must say, Orna, you looked almost as crazy as she did. Alya, standing there like a stranger looking at the sky, smiling... I thought I'd die. My god, Orna, she's mad... really crazy.

Shut up, Orna hissed. Just shut up. Recalling that conversation, Orna suddenly felt, as she had felt many times, and especially since Gill's death, that she had to protect Alya against herself. I should have found a way to prevent her from going to the woods. How could I have been so blinded by jealousy? How? How? And then finally came the tears, tears that had choked her throat that entire day, that entire year. At that moment, like many she had experienced during the war, the world seemed to her dim and grim and menacing—full of evil, infested with demons. I must go to the woods, she cried. I must go to the woods now! And with her eyes still full of tears, she ran out the door and toward the gate of the kibbutz, where Amos, Alya's dog, was still whining, but again to no avail. Ignoring the dog, Orna studied the gate for a moment, then turned around. She decided to go through the olive grove. It was a bit faster to reach the woods that way, but the ground was still muddy from recent rain, and her feet sunk into the wet earth, slowing her pace. Above her, the olive trees stretched their bare branches, motionless, like dark arms. She could still hear the dog's mournful whine, and trying to suppress a feeling of sudden dread, she began to whistle and hastened her pace until she reached the old acacia trunk where she crouched to observe.

Leaning against the Kissing Stone, bathed in the last glow of the red evening light, they looked like images in a dream. Alya was talking, and Ari was listening. The red anemone laurel was around Alya's neck, and her mouth was curved in an enchanted smile. Orna knew well that look of rapture on her friend's face. Oh no, Orna whispered, don't talk about Gill. Please, please, Alya; don't talk about Gill. Would she ever be able to let him go? Would things ever be the way they used to be? Is my happy childhood over, Orna asked herself in a whisper? Yes, it's really over, she answered herself with bitter finality. Her depression, her suffering... time alone would be the healer. Time, she wondered?

When she saw Alya remove the anemone laurel from around her neck and place it, with so much reverence, at the edge of the blanket, Orna understood the significance behind that gesture. She sang softly in a halting, broken voice, Red, red anemones . . .

Behind the top of the trees, the red sun lolled westward. The dusk deepened. Only a trace of twilight lingered in the sky. Rain clouds were gathering; the tops of the cypresses waved restlessly. As the night advanced, it grew cold. Orna shivered. She felt cramped in her hiding place. Slowly she began to rise, when somewhere nearby she heard the branch of a tree snap suddenly. She crouched back. Did I hear footsteps, someone breathing? Must be one of the soldiers. She waited. Nothing. Only the breeze playing, moving through the treetops, scuffing the grass, and birds calling out as they settled for the night. How dumb of me to be so jumpy. I should watch out for my own wild imagination. She leaned her face against the rough bark of the old acacia and gazed into the long shadows of the woods.

Suddenly she went rigid. Two flickering black eyes were staring into hers with a grisly grin of malice. Orna screamed. She leapt up. Her face distorted with terror, she ran toward the Kissing Stone. Ari caught her as she stumbled and almost fell. She clung to him, howling and babbling incoherently. She heard Alya's urgent voice. Orna! What are you doing here? What is it? Orna let go of Ari, and looked at Alya with horror-stricken eyes. There—she pointed to the old acacia, her teeth chattering—I . . . I saw something evil . . . A man . . . A demon with murder in his eyes . . . There . . . there . . . I saw the devil. There is danger in the woods; terrible danger. Let's get out of here before we're dead.

Alya took her friend's hands. She said, Orna, Orna, no one is there. See, Ari is looking behind the acacia tree. Look, he's coming back. All you saw were the shadows of trees and flowers and animals. Calm down. Calm down. Orna released her breath, but the horror lingered in her eyes. This place gives me the creeps, it's so spooky. I am sure I saw something. And leaning her trembling arms on the Kissing Stone, she hid her face in her hands. Alya, she sobbed, I was so jealous, and then suddenly I had the feeling that something awful is going to happen to you. Really, I'm so ashamed for the lunatic way I've behaved. She looked at Ari. His face was pale and very silent, but she saw no surprise on his face, no confusion. She tried to smile. Ari put his hand on her shaking shoulder. Don't cry, don't cry, Orna. It's all right now. You had a bad fright. It's really all right. He turned to Alya. It will be completely dark soon. Let's go back.

But looking beyond them, far into the woods, Alya saw a soldier approaching. Look, Alya cried and pointed. It's only a soldier after all. Only a soldier, she whispered to herself faintly. Orna wheeled around, and still crying, and at the same time laughing hysterically, she waved her arms frantically. Let's go, Ari said. Now! He was looking in the direction of the old acacia. His face tightened with sudden tension. But Alya didn't seem to see or hear him. She merely stood and listened to the woods. The soldier raised both arms and waved back; and as he ran toward them, his machine gun swung to his side, its metal glittering red in the fading twilight. What's going on? What are you doing in the woods? The soldier's voice was low and angry. We're going back, Ari said. Then hurry. A look passed between the soldier and Ari. The soldier made a signal with his head in the direction of the old acacia, and Ari acknowledged it with a slight nod of his head; then he caught Alya's hand. Come on, let's go; quick! She was startled by the sudden sharpness of his voice but went with him without resisting.

The soldier grabbed Orna's arm. I'll walk with you to the edge of the woods, he said in the same low, angry voice. Let go. You're hurting me. Orna tried to free her arm. The soldier ignored her and walked with rapid, almost-running strides, pulling her roughly. They were only a short distance from the Kissing Stone when the shooting began. The soldier cursed. Run! he cried and pushed Orna toward

Ari and Alya. She stumbled. Ari caught her by the hand. They saw the soldier swing around and fire in the direction of the old acacia. They saw him fall. They heard him hit the ground. Get down behind the Kissing Stone! Ari shouted. They ran back amidst a spray of bullets ricocheting—whistling all around them, lodging in the bark of trees, bouncing off rocks, hitting the ground. Shots exploded everywhere. Shots and shouts. Hell.

Alya stopped running and stood rooted to the earth. Her face was lifted; and her eyes were staring, as if in a trance, far into the darkening sky above her head. Still running, Orna turned her head. She screamed, Alya! Get down! But Alya didn't move. Oh my god! Alya! Orna almost reached her friend when a bullet struck her between her shoulder blades. She leaped forward and hit the Kissing Stone. Three more bullets entered her body, painting her white sweater dark purple. On the flat surface of the stone, she lay facing the sky, her blue eyes wide-open. And her face... her face was that of the child she so yearned to be.

Ari stumbled. His body struck the moist ground. With his fingernails, he clawed the earth and, with his last breath, dragged himself to where Alya lay. He collapsed at her side, his head barely touching her right shoulder. He felt his head burning, blood blinding his eyes. To touch her face. Can't move... Can't see. It's so dark. The clamor in his head was unbearable. He vomited. Then relief. No pain. Silence. Dan... Dan?

At the foot of the Kissing Stone, Alya was lying on her back, her fingers moving, caressing the silky grass. With feverish eyes, she watched the fog descend over the tops of the trees, slowly, enveloping the universe with a halo of light. And through the light, a voice called:

Come, let us go for a heavenly walk.

She lost consciousness. After a while, she awoke dizzy with pain. What's happening? Where was she hit? Was this blood? Was it really the end? What was this smell in the air? Rain? Was it rain on her face? She tried to move her legs. Impossible. Her hand groped around. Her fingers touched Ari's head. She summoned all her willpower and lifted herself up, supporting her trembling body on her left elbow. She looked down at his inert face. Ari, she whispered, Ari. His eyes were staring at the sky. With her right hand, she touched his cheeks. His face was still warm, his flesh still firm. Was it blood on her hand?

Now, so easy to break the cord of life. Now, a little push, a last breath, a mere glide from here to there. She collapsed. The silence and darkness were heavy around her. She was sinking fast. Suddenly, behind her closed eyelids, a blast of light. She opened her eyes. Lightning. The air was flushed with lightning, the sky white. I want to live. I want to live, her mind screamed. Orna, she called! Orna! Somewhere in the woods, a night bird screamed.

She pushed herself up again. She turned her head. She saw Orna lying on the Kissing Stone, the growing darkness falling, shrouding her body layer by layer, like gauze. Her face, illuminated by the lightning, looked ghostly. Orna. Orna. Alya lost her courage. She lay still, mad with pain. To sleep. Not to know. So much fear. Gill. Gill.

Don't be afraid. I'm here. It's only a bad dream. Here, that's better. Nothing bad will happen to my little girl. Shhh. Tomorrow will be a beautiful day, says Gill.

Suddenly she smiled, and in a clear voice she said, Good-bye, Gill. She closed her eyes. Ari. Orna. Gill. Orna, Orna. Orna. Don't tell on me, Orna. Please don't tell on me. She heard voices. Familiar voices. A dog bark. I can't. Hurry. Hurry.

She fainted and awoke, and again fainted. After some time, when her own screams pulled her back from the night into semiconscious numbness of the cold and pain, she saw, like in a dream, the wind torches coming near. She heard voices and barks. She felt hands lifting her up. Faces swayed above her, blurred masks. Something warm and wet on her face. A dog whined.

And the last thing she was aware of before she sank back into the dark was the fragrance of the rain, the pines, and the wet earth.

(from the collection after the war)

ANEMONES

Part 1

(Her Father)
The silence was at its deepest, the stillness undisturbed, the crickets ceased their racket; night-watchmen slept their guard and the anemones, red, red anemones sang to the girl in the bedroom where she rested in solitude.

Obeying an inner command, she rose up from her bed. Night-clothed. She went to stand at the door that she had opened.

Anemones... red, red anemones sang to the girl in the bedroom where she rested in solitude.

For a moment, she stood listening, then closed the door behind her and walked into the night, more like floating on moonbeams, expecting no answer.

Anemones... red, red anemones sang to her solitude.

Down the moonlit path, toward the old water tower, where, a few weeks gone past, five corpses of soldiers lay on the ground wrapped in blood-stained army blankets.

Anemones... red, red anemones sang to her solitude.

Time leapt back. She saw the corpses, stretched out, their naked feet protruding, ghost- like in the moonlight.

I am dreaming, and my eyes can see . . .Anemones... red, red anemones,

She bent down, lifted the blankets searched the faces; with the tips of her fingers. She, extraordinarily softly, touched the faces.

Anemones... red, red anemones sang to her solitude.

He wasn't there. Gill! she called. Gill! She began walking around the bodies just as she had walked then—that day; the day they'd brought the bodies.

Red, red anemones

Then, she heard Gill's voice, soft and clear and bright. Tomorrow will be a beautiful day. Go to the woods. To our secret place. Yes, yes. Tomorrow.

In the woods, our secret place. yes.

Listen, Gill, I've something to tell you . . . anemones... red, red anemones . . .

Gill was gone. The corpses vanished. She alone was standing by the old water tower, smiling at nothing. She returned to her room singing Gill's favorite tune, anemones... red, red anemones . . .

She went on singing, even softer, as she got into her bed. For a while, she lay quietly, her eyes wide-open.

Anemones... red, red anemones sang to her solitude.

She remembered the sky; black. Each star a burning flame; the moon bigger, brighter than ever. The moss sprouting out of cracks in the cement of the old water tower. The smell of death on the soldiers' faces.

Anemones... red, red anemones sang to her solitude.

Then the night silkened and only Gill's voice lingered in her mind, lulling her to sleep.

Anemones... red, red anemones sang to her solitude.

Part two

When people mentioned the war or talked of death, a hard and remote expression would invade her face, leaving her brilliant brown eyes expressionless. She would walk way.

Look for me in the orchard; watch for me in the vineyard.

Her friends would watch her with apprehension. A surge of pain rose to their chests. They would follow her silently watching her pale, little face. And they would swallow their tears.

Look for me in the orchard,

Watch for me in the vineyard.

Everyone talked about the war— that was all they have been talking about. More often than not, instead of going to school, she would go to the woods, or the olive grove, sit under a tree and read-

Look for me in the orchard, watch for me in the vineyard.

Mostly she dreamed of her walks with Gill through fields, orchards, olive groves.

Look for me in the orchard, watch for me in the vineyard.

Sometimes her mother would find her fast asleep, her face buried in a bunch of yellow dandelions that grew in abundance under the trees.

Look for me in the orchard, watch for me in the vineyard.

She would sit next to her, stroking her daughter's hair. Alya would say that school was boring; she was so happy in the woods and the grove.

Don't be angry mama, please. Look for me in the orchard, watch for me in the vineyard.

If anyone asked her mother where her daughter was, her mother would shrug her shoulders, impatiently. What do you want? Leave her alone. At times she wished to scream at her daughter; Gill is dead. He was killed in the war, and will never come back.

Look for me in the orchard, watch for me in the vineyard.

But she merely took her daughter, squeezing her into her breast. Then she would go to the kitchen and put supper on. Her daughter's growing remoteness was excruciating for her to bear.

Look for me in the orchard, watch for me in the vineyard.

Alone. Sometimes in the dead of night, she hears her dead man say,

Look for me in the orchard, watch for me in the vineyard. I will come to you when the apple has ripened, even if I have to brake hell.

CHAPTER 20

In The Army

AND IN ISRAEL, WE HAD TO JOIN THE ARMY for two years.

I, a little ballerina, with a gun, wearing army uniforms, stationed in the Arava Desert, teaching war to young men.

Liat looks at her watch. Almost midnight, she whispers to herself. Time to dream again, to dream about the thrill she had then in that desert. This excitement, which is like a drug in my blood. A perpetual desire to play with death. I spend hours fantasizing, re-enacting, reliving every moment of that day. It was as though my body has a memory of its own, and the year is still 1953, and the summer rules over sky and sea, growing out of control and spreading itself all over space into lunatic dimensions. And I am eighteen years old, serving my term in the army, six months into a special training course for military instructors in a camp that used to be a British barrack, perched on a hill by the Mediterranean with the ruins of the gray cement buildings still scattered all over the beach like giant seashells. During the day, the place was dazzling with the white beach below the hill and the low waves lazily foaming and softly purring. And above the sea, the sky, so blue, stretching out to infinity. And in these magical surroundings, I trained all day and often at night, with the sea breeze always chasing after me.

All seemed possible when I was eighteen—strong, full of ideals, and so enthusiastic. We trained hard, men and women together. We did almost everything together, but slept in separate barracks, which wasn't a big problem because about ten minutes after lights-out, I would sneak onto the beach and meet my boy friend among the ruins of the old British buildings, and swim naked in the rustling, rolling, welcoming sea. Once I was caught and had to stay after training in the barracks for a week. It meant no entertainment and no freedom to move about the camp; that was a little rough. My boyfriend at that time was Danny Oren, one of the officers... a vain and fatuous man, but absolutely gorgeous, as they say in America. It was all so stimulating, so new, and the summer lasted forever and smelled of sea and sand and innocence, and everyone was all tanned and beautiful and looked as if drenched in honey. My face was painted with freckles as big as copper coins, and there was a lot of gold in everyone's hair and in the air, so much gold that even the moon seemed golden instead of silver. And we never slacked off on our training.

The competition was fierce. Everyone had to be the first, the bravest, the fastest, and the strongest. Every one of us wanted to be the best. I was the best sharpshooter— excuse the boast. I won a medal, and my name was mentioned in the newspapers as the only female competitor among hundreds of men. It was fantastic. My ego was inflated to the point of bursting. Everything seemed possible then, and I was going to live forever. And then suddenly and without warning, the summer was over, and so was the training course—and the fun. Even the sky and the sea seemed duller. I was made a Corporal and said good-bye to Danny Oren, solemnly, promising never to forget him, and yes, yes, of course I'd write. I'd write to everyone.

The next day, I boarded a bus heading to the desert city of Beer-Sheba, where I was to be stationed. My assignment was to train a group of young men, before they reached the age of eighteen and went into the service. The idea was that they would be prepared when they joined the regular army and would save time in basic training. And so I was stationed in Beer-Sheba and assigned to work in a new village inhabited by Moroccan Jews and situated in the Arava desert, about five miles north of the city. I was briefed about the job by my new commanding officer, a small compact man in his early thirties, immaculately dressed, who even in the worst heat carried himself erect, as small people sometimes do in order to give an impression of being bigger than they actually are. Two days after I arrived in Beer-Sheba. he drove me to the village to meet the group of boys I was to train.

And in the jeep on the way to the village, I remember him watching me with a look I couldn't quite fathom at the time. One minute his forehead would crease with worry, and he would shake his head. Then he would chuckle to himself and look as if he had remembered a joke he wouldn't share with anybody. As we approached the village, he looked less amused and more apprehensive, and I felt nervous too. The mystery was soon over. We arrived at the village, which consisted only of a few wooden huts and some anemic-looking desert shrubbery. On one porch, a few old men were playing backgammon and drinking arak from filthy glasses. It was siesta time, so apart from them the place seemed deserted. But as I jumped off the jeep, I saw a group of young men standing by a water tower, yelling and laughing and shoving one another, looking like mental patients, escaped from an asylum.

Here they are, my commanding officer said. He approached the boys and told them to get in line, which they did reluctantly, grumbling. They were dirty and sloppy, their bodies exuding an overwhelming odor of sweat and garlic, and something else that I couldn't identify just then—later I became familiar with the taste and smell of hashish. And when my commanding officer introduced me as Corporal Liat Erez, their new instructor, a sudden silence fell over the entire group, as if a machine gun had suddenly stopped firing. They stood gaping at me, uncomprehending, yet curious, with sort of a weird, black-browed amusement, as apes in a zoo gape at visitors. And I stood facing them not sure what to say, or how to handle the situation, because this wasn't the army, and I couldn't have expected to be obeyed by giving orders. I knew I had to gain their trust and make them like and respect me, but I felt utterly confused, as if I had lost myself in a blinding labyrinth and couldn't find my way out. They were big and dark and rough-looking, in kind of a cocky, shabby way. I looked at my commanding officer for help, but he only shrugged as if to say, they're all yours.

So I said, Shalom, and hoped for the best. I asked the first boy on the left, a small thin creature with crooked rust-colored teeth and tiny deep-set eyes that glittered like new thumbtacks, his name. Didi, he said, and they all burst into uncontrollable laughter, shoving and poking one another, while Didi danced around looking like a mad thing in the night. Then a tall dark boy with oily black curls and wild eyes smiled at me crookedly. What is it, a kindergarten? What do I see, a little girl? How old are you, sweetie, ten... twelve? He said all this in a creamy voice, and through puckered lips he blew little kisses in my direction. The boys doubled over, shrieking like lunatics. All I wanted was to stop their laughter and this unexpected mockery of my authority. I wanted to smash that smiling face into tiny pieces and grind the pieces into the dust with my foot, but I didn't move. I stood erect in front of them, determined to win the moment, and asked the dark boy his name. He only continued to smile. I strove to find words to save my honor, but all the clever words I had rehearsed vanished from my brain, evaporated into the boom of the desert heat. It felt as if I were watching a play, yet being inside it at the same time. I remember thinking, am I dreaming this?

Finally, unable to think of anything, I shouted, Shut up! Just shut up! To my surprise, the tall one with the oily curls stopped smiling and slowly straightened himself up. He fixed his eyes on me with a long, penetrating look. I held my head high and glared back. I saw that the boys stopped laughing and stood motionless. Only Didi broke every now and then into what sounded like a shriek, but he stopped immediately after a look from the tall boy with the oily curls.

I am Emil, the boy said, and I saw him look at his hands. The fingernails were bitten and bloody, and the hands were filthy. As if embarrassed, he rubbed them on the sides of his torn jeans. Emil, I said. Yes, he said and again gave me his brilliant smile. I'm appointing you to be in charge of this group. Now get everyone in line. I want to talk to all of you. And Didi mimicked me, Yah, Emil. Yah, yah. She wants to talk to you. And I heard Emil say, Shut up, Didi, but his voice was deep with affection. I didn't feel half as sure as I hoped I sounded. I felt dirty and crumpled. My hair was sticky and damp and stuck out from under my cap, pricking my neck. And I was dripping with perspiration. All I wanted was to go home and take a bath. These boys were far from anything I had ever known, so poor and primitive—almost illiterate, utterly undisciplined. To me, born and raised in Kibbutz Regev, they existed only in stories or in movies. Who was I to walk into their lives? I had to remind myself constantly that I was a soldier in the Israeli army, and these boys were my responsibility.

Once Emil got the group in line, they stood ill at ease, some kicking at little stones on the ground, others scratching their heads, and some only standing awkwardly with their hands in their pockets, looking at me blankly. No one laughed, not even Didi, and I wasn't sure I liked it. I heard the wind whine, and I shivered.

Then Emil said, Commander Liat, we are ready. And as he stood at attention—saluting me with his pelvis and belly thrust out, his shoulders hunched, his chest caved in—he looked so comical. It was my turn to laugh. Yet at that moment, looking at him, I was aware of a floating sensation, a fascination. At the same time, I noticed that all of the buttons on his shirt, except one, were missing, so I didn't laugh. I stood staring at him for a long time, probably holding my breath, for I remember feeling dizzy. He just stood there and continued to smile at me brilliantly, perhaps a little mockingly. I wasn't sure; I wasn't sure of anything. The heat was so intense I felt as if I were melting.

I suspected that Emil was making fun of me when he saluted me in such a theatrical way. Yet from that time on, he called me Commander Liat. Later he said that it made him feel good to call me commander and that it gave me importance. Don't be offended, he said, if we call you commander, you look much bigger and more important—even if you are only a girl. Soon the boys came to the training sessions dressed in clean clothes, their hands and faces scrubbed. They quickly learned to drill and to use different weapons, but their favorite time was the night training, orientation by the stars. We had such a good time, lots of laughs and rapport. Everything was going great. And after a while, I even got used to Didi and came to like him.

Didi was Emil's shadow. Where Emil went, Didi went. What Emil said, Didi repeated. Didi had been orphaned when he was ten years old. He didn't have brothers or sisters. He didn't have anyone. And Emil had convinced his mother to let Didi come live with their family. It didn't really matter, Emil had said, because there are thirteen of us, and one more wouldn't make any difference. It didn't take much to convince his mother. And so Didi moved in with Emil's family and became one of the clan.

Sometimes I would visit Emil's mother. I would sit in the shade of her neat little hut drinking spicy tea, brewed especially for me, and we would talk. When I asked her about Didi, she said that after a while, she didn't even remember that Didi wasn't her own child. But sometimes—when Didi behaved completely nuts, as she put it—she would forget herself and say, I don't believe I gave birth to such an ugly thing, and then she would remember and squeeze Didi into her gigantic bosom, and with tears in her eyes, she would say that she loved him as much as she loved her own children. But it wasn't Didi she was concerned about. It was Emil.

He's very wild, she would say. Wild like a big black animal. He gets into much trouble; much trouble. You talk to him. He thinks you okay. She would say this in a kind of a stage whisper, and looking at me in a conspiratorial way, she would shake her head and click her tongue and spit against the evil eye. Emil was everyone's favorite. The people in the village idolized him, perhaps also feared him a little—feared the toughness of his manners, his raw and, at times, violent temper. When people didn't know him, they could never decide how to take him, and yet they loved him—and so did I.

But things weren't as smooth as all that, and all wasn't as wonderful as I in my enthusiasm and naïveté was determined to believe then. Boys from different villages around Beer-Sheba formed gangs and fought one another, and sometimes the fights were so fierce they were severely injured. Instructors were strictly forbidden to go alone at night to the villages, and we didn't carry weapons with us like other soldiers. We went to the villages in pairs; an army truck would take us from Beer-Sheba to the village and return a few hours later to pick us up. But at almost nineteen, I had the illusion that I was immortal. Doesn't everyone at this age?

About two months later, Zaki, my work mate, was ill. And without him, my commanding officer flatly refused to let me go alone to the village. You know the rules, he said. It's out of the question. It's against regulations. Then come with me, I said. You're forgetting yourself, Corporal. Besides, there is an officers' meeting this evening, which makes it impossible for me to go with you. And, he said,

I have no one else to spare. All the instructors are busy. Sorry. He turned to go.

But I refused to take no for an answer. Nothing bad can happen to me, I argued. I am familiar with the desert, and I love the desert. I know it like the palm of my hand—so what's the big deal? I nagged and nagged until finally he gave in with a loud sigh. If anyone can handle the desert, it's you, Corporal Liat Erez. Now go; I see the truck is ready to leave. Go. Even now, I see him standing there, a small, neat man looking at me with his eyebrows raised, his mouth a little open as if he were going to say more. But the truck, with me on it, took off, obscuring him in a whirlpool of gray dust.

During that evening's training session, the boys were strangely silent, but I noticed some peculiar hand movements that looked like secret signals. Quick flashes of the eye darted all around me. Suddenly the night seemed to be filled with whispers. I felt it closing in on me. It was spooky. My nerves were on edge. I asked Emil what was going on, but he merely looked at me and shrugged. Knowing Emil, I left it at that. We finished training early, and I decided to take a short walk by myself. I remember feeling agitated, my nerves still on edge. I wanted to be alone. I would meet the truck on its way to the village. But when I told Emil, he protested. You're not going alone, he said, suddenly looking grim, almost angry. Wait until they come to get you. I laughed and told him not to give me orders and not to worry. I can take care of myself, I said. And besides, I'm only going a little way to meet the truck. He gazed at me in a sort of sulky silence. I noticed a muscle twitching in his cheek. You're worried about something, I said. Not at all, he said. I just don't think it's a good idea. I wondered and was about to change my mind to please him. I didn't. You're always so nervous, I said. I left him standing there, scratching his head, looking sort of miserable.

The night was perfect—the desert waiting, everything present in place, silent—beckoning to me, pulling me like a magnet toward its secrets. The desert haunted my mind. And although the moon was only a half-moon, it was very bright outside, like a white night, almost as bright as day but much softer. You know, one of those nights when the Milky Way flows all around you, and you feel as if you are walking, almost floating inside it, touching the stars with the tips of your fingers. And yet it would be a lie to say that I wasn't affected by my last exchange with Emil, and for a time, his eyes walked in front of me like two black guards.

Suddenly the silence cracked. I heard voices and turned. I felt alarmed because most people from around there knew me. Then I became aware of a mild sense of panic in my chest and began to walk faster. And when the boys caught up with me, one of them grabbed my arm while another put his hand on the nape of my neck. Little girl, he purred. My heart began to beat with great force, and I broke out in sweat. I said to myself, Stay cool, Liat. Stay cool. And I said to them, Hey, guys, what's going on? Who are your instructors? What village are you from?

But they only laughed and began to push and pull me between them, while the other two stood watching with their grinning mouths splitting their faces like two hyenas. Then one of them said, She's this big shot, Liat. She works with Emil's group. Let's show Emil who's king in this desert.

And I said with as much authority and coolness as I could summon at that moment, cut it out if you know what's good for you. But my words, stupid and useless, sounded hollow. The boys only continued to laugh, pinching my cheeks, pulling my hair, while they made strange clicking noises in their throats. Then one of them got hold of my hair from behind and yanked with such force I thought my neck would snap. He glued a garlic-smelling kiss on my lips, and that made me see red, and my adrenaline shot up. I began to fight, and I knew how because it was part of my training. I was fast; that's the advantage of being small and light. But soon I was on the ground, fighting against what seemed to me thousands of hands and legs and lips. And the night didn't seem so bright anymore with my arms pinned to my side and a grinning, menacing face looming above me. I sunk my teeth into hard flesh, and a sharp, sweetish taste filled my mouth. I spat. A boy slapped my face. Someone laughed while someone else was fumbling with my belt buckle. I kicked hard. Someone screamed. A hand was clamped over my mouth, and the world became dark and purple with a million stars falling all around me. Then someone said, I hear something. Let's get out of here. Hurry.

And the Milky Way became clear once more. I stood up trembling with rage, not even bothering to wipe the dirt and blood from my face. I thought of running after them. And then what? What will I do to them? I stood there and screamed, Bastards! You rotten bastards! Just wait. Suddenly I heard a high whistle and Emil's voice shouting, They went the other way! Quick, get them! And Didi's voice echoed, Get them, get them. Emil! I called. Wait! He halted abruptly, his body stiffening, then turned and saw me. Get them! he yelled to the other boys. No! I yelled. Go! he yelled.

The boys ran. Only Didi waited. Emil ran toward me. I ran after the boys, shouting, Come back. Don't start anything. You'll get us in trouble. Come back! Come back! It's an order! But they were oblivious to my existence. Emil caught up with me. He gripped my arm. Don't interfere, he said through clenched teeth. You shouldn't be here. What happened to your face? And your clothes? You're a mess. What the hell! Where's the truck? I saw his face flush, and his eyes became almost insane with anger.

Obviously, the truck is late, I said, trying to sound nonchalant. And besides, you're hurting my arm. Let . . . But he was looking at me wildly from under dusty curls with eyes narrowed like two black cracks, and he was panting like a dog on a hot day. I saw that his face became very pale, and I felt again that sweet pain between my throat and stomach that grabbed me every time I looked at him. And for a second, our bodies came in close contact, and his breath hit me in the face, and his mouth came down on mine. It was as if for a split second, we were completely alone, and all things seemed to pause and stand still until he let go of my lips. We stepped back from one another, and he cleared his throat and said, Stay here. It's not your fight. And his voice sounded hollow and dark.

Emil! someone called. Coming! And he ran. I ran after him, shouting, Emil, don't. And I heard my voice as a whisper and saw the boys holding razors in their hands, and they hissed and whistled and circled one another like gladiators, and they kept tripping over each other and falling in a tangle then jumping up and circling and whistling and hissing again. I could hardly tell who was who and tried not to lose sight of Emil—he alone mattered, I thought only of him. Emil was the tallest among the whole mad bunch, and Didi was jumping at his side like a mad thing in the night. And it was awful, truly awful, and yet at the same time, terribly exciting.

I too wanted to join the fight and abandon myself to some primordial instinct, some mysterious primitive calling. I too wanted to bite and hit and kick and hiss, even cut and feel and smell the sweat of those crazed bodies. I kept moving in and out of those confusing yet mesmerizing feelings like in a dream where nothing is real, yet all is so vivid. It was incredible. I saw Emil, and he was dark and predatory, and his eyes were narrowed and cold and reflected the light of the stars. And his lips were curled slightly away from his teeth in a savage smile, and Didi was dancing around him, shrieking and lisping and laughing. Then I saw Emil pull out a knife, and I leaped into the air and grabbed his raised hand and jerked at it with all my strength, and the knife fell to the ground. I heard Emil shout, Liat, stay back! And Didi echoed, Stay back, stay back. I screamed, Emil, look out! and threw myself on the ground to get the knife when suddenly I felt a sharp pain, and I knew that someone had slashed my leg.

The next thing I saw was my commanding officer running toward me. I grinned at him stupidly and said, I'm all right. He didn't say a word, but his hands shook as he bandaged my leg. I am sorry, I said. Shut up, Liat, he said. Just shut up. And I did. I saw that the boys were attended to by the four other soldiers from other villages who came with my commanding officer, and I saw Emil standing a few feet away, staring at the sky; I watched the excitement still burning in his eyes and the savage smile still splitting his mouth. And near Emil, gazing at him, stood Didi. He was holding a hand to his right ear, and blood was oozing through his fingers. And then I heard my commanding officer say that we were all under arrest, and the devil took hold of me, and I began to laugh, and my laugh sounded terrible. My commanding officer slapped my face twice and said, take hold of yourself, Corporal. And with tears welling in my eyes, I slowly returned to my senses, to the hellish heat, and to reality. I swallowed and didn't cry.

In the truck on the way to Beer-Sheba, Emil sat between Didi and me. Didi's ear was taped, and he was moaning softly, his eyes never leaving Emil's face, and Emil's right arm around his shoulder. The boys sat among the four soldiers, expressionless. I was grateful that my commanding officer was driving because I couldn't have faced him at that moment. My eyes followed the withered thistles on each side of the dusty road, and my spirit felt withered too.

Once my excitement was gone, I felt ashamed and embarrassed and utterly depleted.

At first, Emil wouldn't look at me. And when he finally did, I saw that the extraordinary wildness had left his face, and his eyes had a gloomy, cold expression. He said, You enjoyed the fight. It was a statement, not a question. I nodded my head and turned my face away from him so he wouldn't see my tears. After a while, his mouth relaxed into a slow smile, and he looked at me with his familiar look of teasing affection. He said that when he had realized that I wasn't going to wait for the truck, he didn't know what to do because they had gotten into a quarrel with another gang and were going to meet that night to settle things as he put it.

How could you do this to me? I said. Why didn't you tell me? He laughed a harsh short laugh and said, you must be joking. It was very stupid of you to walk by yourself. You got us all in trouble, and now they'll send you away to do something safe, and they won't even let you say goodbye to us. You shouldn't have pulled that knife, I said. He looked at me, and his eyes narrowed, and he gave a short snort. Don't be so dumb, he said. If I hadn't pulled out the knife, you could have kissed this whole rotten world goodbye forever.

And that shut me up. For a while we sat there swaying to the bouncing of the truck, avoiding each other's eyes. He stared out at the moonlit desert, and I could see that under his anger was a layer of coldness and an unforgiving distance he had placed between us. You're terribly naive about life, Commander Liat, he said. It's time you grow up because the world isn't as you imagine it to be—wonderful—and, he said wistfully, it'll do you good to learn the facts of real life. He kept glancing at the bloodstained bandage on my leg, and I saw him clench his left hand. In his eyes, I saw something of fear or maybe of shame, but probably I only imagined it.

It's nothing, I said. It doesn't hurt at all. Yah, sure, he said. I saw he didn't believe me, and I had no words to comfort him. I squeezed his hand and noticed his face soften. He looked at me, and I felt as if he were looking into the most secret place in me. For only a second, I felt his hand close on mine; then he pulled his hand away and lowered his eyes. It was as if the entrance to his soul had closed forever. A sense of a terrible loss came over me; I wanted to weep from shame and frustration and love. At that moment, it seemed that everything important in my life was retreating. It felt like in a dream, when the heart strains and you want to scream but you can't utter a sound. I didn't weep because I was Commander Liat, a soldier in the IDF. But at that moment, this thought made me so sick that I hung over the side of the truck and vomited, terrified that the boys would laugh at me. No one even smiled.

When we reached Beer-Sheba, we were taken to the army hospital where they cleaned out the cuts on my face and stitched and bandaged my leg and let me go. But I was confined to my room until a decision was reached about me. For three days, I lay on my bed and stared at the ceiling and thought of Emil. Sometimes I would fall into semi-sleep, and my sleep would be infested with dreams of pits and crawling things, and I would wake up sweating and breathless, my heart palpitating. And at night, unable to sleep, I'd stand by the open window and gaze at the desert's stars and sniff the desert scent of faraway bonfires and hot dust and think of special moments I had shared with Emil, like the night we smoked the hashish, that night when Zaki took the boys for a special night training session. Emil had complained of a migraine headache, and so he and I stayed behind. We sat very close without touching, without words, and watched as the moonlight spread a death mask over the distant hills. Emil was smoking. After a while, he said, Here, take a puff. I don't smoke, I said, and you shouldn't either. I thought you had a headache. But he merely laughed and said, Try, it won't kill you. His voice was hoarse, and his mouth seemed very dry. I took the peculiar-shaped cigarette, inhaled, and almost choked; but Emil didn't laugh.

I want you, he said, but he didn't move. I had no idea what was going to happen next. I felt strange, not unpleasant, as if detached from myself, and very quiet inside. I talked with an effort because my tongue felt somewhat paralyzed. I don't think it's a good idea. It will ruin everything. He didn't answer. He only reached out and took my hands and held them in his, but he didn't make love to me. I sat very still. But he only continued to hold my hands and gaze at me with his eyes half closed, a kind of vacant smile on his face. And that was all we did: looking at each other, smiling, dreaming, and holding hands. Probably looking utterly ridiculous.

Near Tel Aviv, a few months later, I was sitting at my open window, feeling the sea breeze caress my face, breathing the perfume of apple blossoms, watching the night sky above my head, and trying to smile with trembling lips at the cold light of blurred stars that looked as if they were mocking the entire world and especially me. Suddenly the telephone rang. I got up, annoyed and a little frightened. Who could it be at such an ungodly hour? I picked up the phone expecting anyone but the voice of my commander.

Liat? he said. Gideon? I said.

I have bad news.

I sat down on the bed. Liat, are you there?

Where are you? In Beer-Sheba.

Tell me.

He was silent.

Gideon, talk to me.

Emil was rejected by the army. The medical examiner said that he has a mental disorder. At eight o'clock this morning, he shot himself in the head with his brother's gun. He died instantly.

Silence.

Liat?

Yes.

The funeral is tomorrow at four in the afternoon. Shall I pick you up?

Gideon.

Yes?

Thanks. But . . .

I hung up the phone and went back to the window and looked up at the sky. I thought about Emil and how—for only one moment—I felt his heart drumming on my breasts, how his mouth tasted, how it was to smoke hashish. Then I went into the room and sat on the floor and stared at the darkness. My eyes were dry, but I couldn't breathe. I didn't go to the funeral. After three days, Gideon came; and when he took me in his arms, I began to scream, and I screamed and screamed. And Gideon just held me without saying a word. What was there to say? Emil's death was as empty of reason as can be, and I had never even told him how much I wanted him. One wouldn't believe things like that are possible, but it was possible then, and for Emil, perhaps it was the only way.

CHAPTER 21

Gabriela

THERE IS ANOTHER STORY I WISH TO TELL YOU, about someone I will call Gabriela.

When Gabriela came home that evening, she dropped her bag on the couch and walked to the window. Gazing at the oak tree, all she could think about was that day a year ago when she left her father at the hospital in Jerusalem to fly back to Boston to be with her husband, Neil. She remembered how, immediately upon arriving home, she had called her father's doctor. How is he? she asked. Call your mother, Gabriela, he told her. He's dead. Yes, Gabriela, I'm sorry. He died a few hours after you left. For a long moment, she just stood there, clutching the receiver in her hand until her fingers became numb. Vaguely, she heard the doctor's voice say, Gabriela, are you there? Gabriela? All she could think of was that she had to go back to Jerusalem. She didn't unpack or even change her clothes. She didn't call Neil. She called the airlines and took the first flight back to her country. For fourteen hours she sat on the plane, and the only feeling she could remember was a sense of urgency that burned inside her.

When she arrived at her parents' home, it was Friday. Her father's body was at the hospital's morgue. Stunned, she stood at the door. Her father wasn't buried yet and already her parents' home was crowded with people. What are they doing here? A rage filled her brain. She saw her mother moving among the callers, bewildered and exhausted, her skin hanging like a rag on her face, gray rings etched under her eyes, and her hand clutching her chest from time to time as if trying to hush her heart. For a moment, Gabriela felt like a sharp stone had been turned round in her chest, but she wasn't able to attend to her mother. The tremendous feeling of urgency she felt throughout the flight turned into a feeling of suffocation—she must see him now, immediately, to affirm with her own eyes that he was dead, to touch him, to ask his forgiveness for not being there with him in his last moments. The urgency was so great within her she could not lean upon the comforting illusion that she was dreaming and soon she'd wake up. Her friends were shocked when she said she wanted to go to the hospital now. She must have lost her mind. They'll refuse to let her in, they whispered. You can't go now, they cautioned her. Only her cousin, Daniel, a heart surgeon at

Hadassah Hospital, took her hand gently. I'll take you to see him, he said.

At the hospital, she walked along a gray concrete corridor, trembling with pity and anger, refusing to believe the fact that her father had passed through this corridor without her. She hadn't been there as she had promised, and she could make no amends now. She was overwhelmed by a sense of guilt and confusion.

When they reached the morgue, Daniel explained to the attendant that they came to see the body of Michael Wolk. She remembered well the attendant, a small man with a beak-like nose and shoulder-length side curls. A long black coat was hanging on him like on a hanger, and his body emitted the odor of mildew and tobacco. It's forbidden for the woman to be here, he muttered angrily as he plucked at his long black beard. She's my responsibility, Daniel said. The attendant pointed to a wall. He's there, he said sourly. But don't stay long, the Sabbath is coming. I'm closing at four. Please open it. Daniel said. The man pulled at a handle protruding from the wall, and the box glided out soundlessly. Her father's head appeared first, like in birth, she thought. His body was covered with a white sheet. She uncovered his body, baring his chest. Here he is, she heard herself say. She felt as though he was lost and she had just found him. She bent and kissed his forehead, his cheeks, delicately, as if afraid to hurt him. She passed her hand over his face, over his shut eyes, over his slightly opened lips. His skin felt cold to the touch, unnatural, but the feeling was not repulsive to her or even unpleasant. He was her father.

Daniel bent over and carefully opened the dead man's eyes. She gazed into her father's eyes. For a moment, she expected him to say, enough, Gabriela, let's go home. She waited, her hands two blocks of ice. After a while, she rested her cheek on his chest; but when her cheek touched his flesh, she burst out crying. Her entire body shook; chills ran down her spine. She told him she loved him, that she longed for their talks on lazy Sabbath days when he would sit in the soft leather chair and she on the floor, her back leaning on his legs, and his hand would caress her head. She told him how terribly she missed the times they used to spend riding through the flowering hills in winter, breathing the fragrance of wet grass. How she yearned for their walks between the narrow walls of the Arab market in old Jerusalem, inhaling the odors of musky perfumes and ancient spices. She told him how devastated she was not to have been with him when he died.

She talked for a long time. She heard Daniel call her name and felt his hand stroking her hair, and although she could not see him, she knew that he too was crying. Finally, she lifted her head off her father's chest and stood up. She remembered that as the saddest moment of it all, for she knew that now they would close the box, and she would never touch her father again. Full of sorrow, she looked at him. But she was not ready to grieve. Not yet. She did not see death in his still body. She felt rather that he had undergone some shift, some metamorphosis.

Suddenly she saw two tears rolling down his face, leaving a silvery line on each cheek.

Daniel, look, she said, my father is crying. She saw Daniel wince. Let's go, he said and took her hand. But when she lingered, he said, his voice choking, Gabriela, he isn't crying, he's thawing.

She stared at him with huge unblinking eyes. If Jesus could rise from the dead, she said, my father can cry in death. Daniel only smiled and squeezed her hand. At that moment, the attendant came in. He seemed to swoop down upon them, his black coat flying wildly behind him. Dark and mean, he reminded her of a raven. He whispered something in Daniel's ear. Daniel took her hand and said they had to leave now. With her frozen fingers, she wiped her father's tears, then covered his body with the sheet.

On the day of the funeral, she felt quiet and distant. But at night, stunned and lonely, she went back to the cemetery, gathered all the flowers from his grave, and brought them to the house. There she put them, without water, on the floor of his library. During the next seven days, Gabriela looked after her mother. She ran like a maniac between the ringing phone and the screaming doorbell. An endless stream of relatives and people she didn't know came to pay their respects. Many wanted to know how life in America was and whether she was thinking of returning to Jerusalem. It was too bad, they had said, that Neil, her wonderful husband, couldn't come to the funeral; but Gabriela didn't explain. Those most concerned took her aside and wondered how her mother would manage. Maybe it will be better if she were to stay for a few months and take care of her—her husband would surely understand. Gabriela smiled and nodded. Mother will be all right, thank you. It's so sweet of you to be concerned. You're so kind.

The days were chaotic. But at night, after everyone left and her mother took a sleeping tablet; Gabriela would go to her father's library; and there—among his pipes, books, and papers—she lived for a few hours among the aromas of her childhood. Nostalgia, like a drug, coursed through her veins. She sat in the dark, her hands caressing the polished wood of his desk. The windows were open, the night bright, and the scent of the jasmine wafted in with the whine of the jackals. Moonlight poured into the room, casting a blue shadow on the alabaster horse on her father's desk, the winged alabaster horse that always seemed ready to leap toward the sky. Absently, she caressed it, caressed and waited. It took the memorial flowers seven days to wilt.

A year had passed since her father's passing; and now on the anniversary of his death—at her home in Boston, so far from Jerusalem—she leaned her forehead on the windowsill and wept. Yes, she said to the motionless tree as much as to herself, I really believed that he was crying.

At night, she fell on her bed, determined but unable to subdue the pain. She tossed and turned; everything churned within her, shifting like desert sand in a windstorm. Toward dawn, she fell into a deep sleep and dreamed she was a little girl riding on a blue horse, her arms around her father's waist, her cheek pressing against his back. They ride through a field crimson with poppies. Butterflies—purple, yellow, and gold—fly around the horse's legs. A cool breeze plays with her hair, caressing her face. Only father and her, galloping toward the sun, and she is happy and light in the glittering air.

But suddenly the red field becomes a sea of moving shadows. Black clouds sweep the vast expanse of blue sky. She clutches his waist tight, but he pries her arms loose and dismounts. She tries to follow him but is unable. Don't leave me, she cries. How will I find the way in the darkness? I miss you terribly, Father. Please stay.

Gabriela, she hears his voice, don't you remember? I am dead. A tide of darkness sweeps him away. But, Father, she shouts, I didn't bury you, you can't be dead. She is shouting, but her voice is thin, scarcely a thread of a sound. Silence. The only sound she hears is the drumming of her heart. The blue horse gallops through the storm, and she holds tight to its mane. Suddenly the horse stops. Neil, her husband, appears before her. His hands are clasped in prayer, his face gleaming white and wet. I knew you'd come back to me, he whispers. I'm so glad. And she says, No, you're no longer part of my life, I can't stay. A thick mist envelops his face. Gabriela, my wife, we can try again. No! Move out of the way! You're selfish, Gabriela. He continues to weep. You were always selfish. He grabs her hand and tries to pull her off the horse's back, but the blue horse gallops away, and Neil is left cradling her severed hand to his heart. She wants to get off the horse. She wants to retrieve her hand, but the blue horse is flying, floating again in the dark through the storm. She must leave Neil with something. She can do without her hand.

And again the horse halts, scraping its hooves along the ground. Sparks are flying in the darkness. A full moon hangs suspended in space, illuminating the blackness. The face of her lover Paul floats up toward her, radiant in the darkness. Gabriela, he says, I knew you'd come, you always came back to me. No, she says, you left me, you went back to her, you lied to me. He laughs; come to me, my love. We'll be together again, only you and me. His hand is on her chest, squeezing her heart, and an awful sense of suffocation grips her. He tries to pull her off the horse's back. But the blue horse bolts forward, and Paul, her lover, floats in the air with her heart in his hand. I can't help you, she whispers. I must bury my father. Give me back my heart, I can't live without a heart. Gabriela! Gabriela! His rumbling voice is drowned by the howling of the wind and the shrill ringing of bells. Gabriela, you're so selfish, you promised to love me forever. But the horse is flying faster, the wind roars; bells ring.

Father! Father! she shouts and hears his voice. Faster. Don't listen to them, Gabriela. They'd all try to stop you. Go! Go fast! She holds tight to the blue horse's back, and both of them are swirling through endless space.

Sad book. So sorry. But so is life. Moments of pleasure are precious - only moments. Words repeat themselves again and again, muttering, whispering, singing, laughing, shrieking, tripping and disappearing - it seems they won't return, and yet they do come back, tired, a little pale, murmuring in my ear about life being empty bustle, futile, meaningless, their hum fills me with a sense of the hollowness, the inanity of existence in the light of infinite eternity, the banality of space and time. Beyond certainty and uncertainty, the Spirit is undermined. I must finally acknowledge that life - despite those I love and who remain like a lost citadel – is chaos, that I am lost and must adapt to being lost so that I can be saved and feel a pleasurable freshness in my body: elation, and a joyful freedom bordering on a sense of merging with all that exists. I destroy and recreate myself daily. It's exhausting, so exhausting; it generates a spherical, utterly internal feeling of loneliness.

Eric's orchid has withered and, in its place at the window, in all its delicate glory stands my Teddy's orchid which will also wither soon. And you my dearest friend, are there, you are there, and how are things there? Tell me about the skies, the flowers; what do they tell you? Do you see butterflies? I don't, so my smile wrinkles every day. I will end here, my dying swan song, with fond words: like a caressing hand you hover over the tissues of my soul, your laugh illuminates the darkness within me; like a twilight breeze your voice soothes the madness in my blood. You went, because you always go – come back, because you always come back to the place forever reserved for you within me.